AN INTRODUCTION TO ORODISPERSIBLE TABLET

SWAGATIKA DAS

Made with ❤ on the Notion Press Platform
www.notionpress.com

This book dedicated to Aruush and
Deewen

Contents

Preface

Industrial pharmacy is the branch of pharmacy that deals with scientific and technological aspects related to design and development of dosage forms, Pharmaceutical industry is made of hundreds of films involved in discovery, development, production and selling of drug products that meet regulatory requirements. The current curriculum implemented by Pharmacy council of India, New Delhi as Regulation 2014.

This theory book covers whole of the topics specified in the syllabus. The book has been divided five main chapters covering all the aspects related to Pharma industry which include pilot plant Scale-up Techniques. WHO guidelines for technology transfer and various regulatory requirements for Drug approval. All these Chapters have been designed in very easy language, to point coverage of all the topics, in pictorial/graphical manner so that every student can easily understand. After completion of this course students will be able to understand dosage form s and their manufacturing techniques and all the related and practical aspects of dosage form development. This also helps the students to correlate the theoretical knowledge with professional and practical need of pharmaceutical industry.

Taking this as an opportunity, we have tried our level best to give detail insight of the subject expectations with respect to various regularity proccdures followed for the final drug approval and WHO guidelines for transfer of technology. This book is first of it's kind that it covers huge data on manufacturing techniques of various dosage forms. The course is beneficial for teachers, students and the industry personels. Efforts have been taken to elaborate basic concepts of pharmaceutical manufacturing and are supported with flow diagrams, figures, equations and data tables.

Our sincere thanks to Notion publication for their co-operation and continuous support.

Acknowledgements

I would like to express my gratitude to many people who saw me through this boo; to all those who provided support, talked things over, read, wrote, offered comments, allowed me to quote their remarks and assisted in the editing, proofreading and design.

I would lie to thank my mentor, my Father Mr Tappan kumar Das and mother Mrs Gitanjali Das and all teachers of School of Pharmacy, Centurion university who supported and encouraged me constantly

I want to convey my gratitude to the team of Notion publication for their extended support, co-operation and guidance.

CHAPTER ONE

SCOPE AND OBJECTIVES

The oral route of administration continues to be the most popular due to a variety of benefits, including simplicity of consumption, pain avoidance, adaptability, and most significantly, patient satisfaction.. Tablets, capsules, and oral liquid preparations are a few of the numerous dosage forms. There has been an increased need for more patient compliance dose forms during the past 20 years. As a result, especially in the case of elderly, paediatric, or any mentally impaired individuals, these standard dosage forms lead to a high prevalence of noncompliance and ineffective therapy with respect to swallowing. Orodispersible tablets (ODTs) are a highly regarded dosage form because they are simple to administer to the general public, especially to elderly, young, or intellectually impaired individuals. Due to the presence of super disintegrants, it dissolves fast, leading to quick drug absorption and, in turn, a quick commencement of action.

Therefore, many geriatric patients find it difficult to swallow solid dosage forms such as tablets or capsules ease of administration of dosage forms is of paramount importance, especially amongst certain Alzheimer's disease patients who tend to be even less cooperative. In recent years, various novel drug delivery systems have been developed to improve patient compliance.

The primary scope of the research is to prepare and evaluate orodispersible Galantamine HBr, Memantine HCl and Donepezil HCl tablets to overcome the limitations of ordinary tablet formulation.

Objectives

To achieve the primary aim following objectives have been set:

1. To authenticate the pure drugs (Galantamine HBr, Memantine HCl and Donepezil HCl) using non-thermal method.

2. To select and optimize the best formulation based on *in vitro* release study.

3. To achieve speedy dissolution of drug and absorption which may produce quick onset of action for selected drugs by *in vitro* release study.

4. To carry out physico chemical evaluation tests for the formulations developed such as weight variation, thickness, hardness, friability, weight variation, wetting time, disintegration test and drug content uniformity.

5. To perform preformulation studies such as bulk density, tapped density compressibility index, Hausner's ratio and angle of repose to find the flow properties for prepared granules.

6. To design and develop orodispersible tablets for the selected drugs (Galantamine HBr, Memantine HCl and Donepezil HCl) using suitable approach by selected method.

7. To study the compatibility between drugs and various ingredients to be used in the proposed orodispersible

formulations.

8. To select a suitable method for the preparation of orodispersible tablets using the Analytical Hierarchy Process (AHP).

9. To assess kinetic modelling of selected formulation

10.To evaluate the bioavailability parameters of the prepared galantamine HBr, memantine HCl and donepezil HCl tablets using Wistar rats as animal model.

11. To carry out accelerated stability studies for optimized formulations as per ICH guidelines.

12.To carry out comparative study between the optimized formulations from each drug with marketed formulation.

CHAPTER TWO

INTRODUCTION

Introduction

Despite significant advancements in medication delivery methods such parenteral, transdermal, nasal, etc., the oral route of administration is still the most preferred method. (Gauri and Kumar, 2012). This is a result of its many benefits, including simplicity of consumption, reduced pain, exact dosage, opportunity for self-medication, adaptability, and, most importantly, patient compliance. (Rajeev *et al.*, 2013). It is the most popular method of medication delivery and is typically regarded as the most practical and cost-effective due to the fact that it is the least expensive. (Bardelmeijer *et al.*, 2000).

These qualities have led to a high level of patient acceptability of the oral route, which accounts for between 50 and 60 percent of all potential dosage forms.. However, some medications can irritate the digestive system. One of the fundamental issues with this dosage type is that regular tablets are difficult to swallow. Additionally, swallowing problems and inconveniences are often experienced by paediatric and geriatric individuals. Since drinking water is essential for properly swallowing oral dose forms, patients who are suffering from conditions like motion sickness or other conditions where water is not readily available may find it difficult to swallow the tablet. (kinetosis), abrupt coughing fits with a cold, an allergic reaction, or bronchitis. These factors have led to a lot of interest in tablets that can quickly dissolve or disintegrate in the oral cavity. (Prabhakar *et al.*, 2012).

Orodispersible tablets (ODTs) are solid single-unit dosage forms that are meant to be placed in the mouth without the use of water before being ingested. The tablet will instantly disperse or dissolve in the saliva, taking only a few seconds, and can then be easily swallowed as residue. The absorption and start of a therapeutic effect happen more quickly the faster the medications dissolve and disintegrate. There are also various solid oral dosage forms that can be administered without drinking any water, such as lozenges, buccal, and chewable tablets. The way the drugs are released, however, varies between them. Lozenges, buccal tablets, and ODTs are designed to dissolve gradually in the mouth, whereas chewable tablets take longer to dissolve and must first be chewed by the patient before they can be ingested. Over the past three decades, ODTs have supplanted traditional oral dosage forms like tablets, capsules, and other liquid medicinal preparations as a preferred option. Some names that have been used as synonyms for orodispersible tablets include rapidly disintegrating tablets, fast dissolving tablets, mouth dissolving tablets, melt in the mouth, fast dissolving drug administration, and quick dissolving tablets. Orodispersible tablets was the phrase recognilsed by the European Pharmacopoeia. They described it as a tablet that is swallowed after being quickly dissolved in the mouth. (Sreenivas *et al.*, 2005).

ODT tablets, as defined by the USFDA, are solid dosage forms containing medications that dissolve quickly when placed on the tongue, typically in a couple of seconds. Because of their practicality and ease, ODTs have statistically been shown to have a number of advantages over traditional tablets in terms of improving patient compliance and adoption. Nearly 50% of the populace while ingesting tablets and firm gelatin capsules, has trouble swallowing

These groups of people include children and the elderly who have trouble swallowing big tablets. Orodispersible tablets (ODT) and mouth dissolving tablets (MDT) have been created as substitute oral dose forms to address these issues. (Dixit *et al.*, 2012).

ODTs became a great option as a new drug delivery method as a result since they are simple to use and improve patient compliance, especially in the case of the old and young patients. Even energetic persons without any swallowing issues find orodispersible tablets to be highly appealing. Fast dissolving pills must be packaged in specialised peel off blisters due to their extreme fragility. ODT technology have advanced very quickly over the past ten years. To address the shortcomings of prior products, new generations of ODT have been developed. Some businesses used cutting-edge technology to create palatable tablets to solve the widespread issue of poor medicine taste, which reduced the benefits of ODTs. In order to enhance the regulated release of ODTs, other businesses created additional technologies. Fast-dissolving tablets are simpler to make and carry less dangers, therefore ODT technology is a great option for the majority of pharmaceutical manufacturing. The only mode of administration for ODTs is orally, which further contributes to their great favorability. Due to this one aspect, other businesses can obtain permission for a generic version of the medication. (Ghosh *et al.*, 2011).

Criteria for orodispersible tablets (Modi A *et al*, 2006**)**

1. ODTs can be consumed with or without water because they dissolve or disintegrate in the mouth within a matter of seconds.

2. They work well with flavour masking and other excipients.

3. ODTs leave little to no aftertaste in the tongue and have a nice mouthfeel.

4. This can be very helpful in order to avoid the bitter taste of the drugs, particularly for pediatric patients.

5.ODTs offer good stability since they are less sensitive to environmental factors

Desirable characteristics of orodispersible tablets (Bradoo R *et al*, 2001)

- ODTs display some perfect qualities that set them apart from other dosage forms, including traditional tablets. Some of these significant desirable characteristics include the following:
- Effective cost because it is less expensive to produce, package, and distribute than other commercially accessible products.
- Convenient to administer, especially for children and elderly patients who refuse to swallow, as well as other populations who would have trouble taking typical oral dosage forms, like the mentally challenged, stroke sufferers, bedridden patients with renal failure, and recalcitrant patients.
- sufficient strength to withstand the rigours of manufacture and handling after manufacturing

- Since they are units of solid dosage forms, which allow for maximum drug loading and are an excellent solution for children and geriatric patients, they provide accurate dosing in comparison to other dose forms like liquids.
- Has a rapid onset of action which will produce fast dissolution and absorption of the drug in the oral cavity.

Common conditions for ODTs indications (Rani Thakur R *et al*, 2012)

Pain, fever, heartburn, diarrhea, migraine, anxiety, insomnia for fast faction.

Parkinson's disease, Alzheimer's disease, psychosis, Schizophrenia, Hypertension, cholesterol, transplantation to improve patient's compliance

Cough, cold, allergy, pain, fever, ADHD that can be associated with pediatrics.

Advantages of ODTs as drug delivery system (Shu T et al, 2002 and Chang RK, 2000)

Pregastric absorption from the mouth, pharynx, and esophagus as the saliva passes down into the stomach can result in enhancement of bioavailability which leads to a reduced dosage and improves the clinical performance and reduces the side effects.

It is useful for some conditions that need a rapid action such as motion sickness, sudden episodes of allergic attack or coughing.

Highly convenient for patients who are traveling anywhere, anytime and do not have instant access to water.

Provide a suitable drug delivery for some drugs that have low molecular weight and are highly permeability.

Cost effective for manufacturing because they require a minimum number of ingredients .

Due to rapid disintegration and dissolution time, orally dissolving tablets increase the bioavailability of insoluble and hydrophobic drugs.

Improve patient safety administration by avoiding the risk of chocking or suffocation during oral administration due to physical obstruction.

Limitation of orodispersible tablets

ODTs have a unique feature by combining the advantage of solid and liquid dosage forms. They provide long term stability for the solid dosage form and high bioavailability as a liquid dosage form when placed on the mouth.

Useful for pediatric, geriatric and psychiatric patients because there is no need for chewing.

Medications with a bitter taste have taken advantage of ODTs technologies by the use of flavours and sweeteners to make them as pleasing as possible when they dissolve in the mouth.

The new ODTs patented technologies allow the incorporation of microencapsulated drugs for enhanced bioavailability, flexibility of dosing and immediate and/or controlled release.

As ODTs are unit solid dosage forms, they provide ease of handling by the patients.

ODTs technologies show multipurpose utilization; therefore they are suitable for the development of enhanced products for veterinary medicines, OTC, as well as prescription medicines.

Orodispersible tablet technologies have been expanded to provide a new business opportunity demonstrating product differentiation, product promotion, patent extensions and life cycle management.

Insufficient mechanical strength that make ODTs difficult to handle.

Some of ODTs may leave unpleasant taste or gritty feel in the mouth if they not formulated properly.

Drug selection criteria (Kumaresan C *et al*, 2008)

Dose should be lower than 20 mg for FDT.

Drug should be partially nonionized at pH in oral cavity.

Drug should be diffuse and partition into the epithelium of the upper GIT (log P > 1, or preferably >2)

Drug should have to permeate through oral mucosal tissue.

Ideal drugs which are used in ODTs(Shailesh Sharma *et al,* 2008)

Analgesic and Anti-Inflammatory Agents: Ibuprofen, Proxicam, Mefenamic Acid

Anti-bacterial Agent: Erythromycin, Tetracycline, Doxycycline.

Anti-fungal Agents: Griseofulvin, Miconazole

Anti-Malarial: Chlorquine, Amodiaquine

Anti-Gout Agent: Allopurinol, Probenecid

Anti-Hypertensive: Amlodipine, Nefidipine

Anti-Coagulants: Glipizide,Tolbutamide

Anti-Protozoal Agents: Benznidazole, Tinidazole

Anti-Thyroid agent: Carbimazole

Cardiac Inotropic Agent: Digitoxin, Digoxis

Gastro-Intestinal Agents: Omeprazole, Ranitidine, Famotidine

Nutritional Agents: Vitamin A, Vitamin B, Vitamin D etc

Oral Vaccine: Influenza, Hepatitis, Polio, Tuberculosis etc

First generation ODTs

Since they are units of solid dosage forms, which allow for maximum drug loading and are an excellent solution for children and geriatric patients, they provide accurate dosing in comparison to other dose forms like liquids. In the pharmaceutical industry, it had great success. However, it didn't take long for the pharmaceutical industry to learn that some medications cannot be taken in ODT dosage form. To choose ODTs, for instance, the amount of active pharmaceutical ingredient (API) should be minimal. The scientists' hunt for a unique technology that can adapt and address some of the problems associated with the first generation was made possible by this and other challenges.

High porosity, low density, and low hardness are some of the key characteristics of first-generation ODTs, making them fragile and challenging to handle. ODT produced by freeze drying are extremely friable, making conventional packaging quite challenging and requiring significant thought for storage stability. The harsh taste of first-generation medicines is another drawback. Traditional flavouring and sweetening chemicals were shown to be particularly ineffective at masking the bad taste, which limits their use. These days, there are various cutting-edge technologies available on the pharmaceutical market that can effectively disguise tastes. Coacervation (encapsulation) technology is one of the technologies available on the market. Pharmaceutical companies want to make better use of ODT dosage forms. By addressing the problems of the prior generation, such as increased API loading, more

Effective taste muffling, controlled release capabilities, minimal friability, economical development, and a wider range of packaging alternatives.

New generation ODTs (Shukla D et al, 2009)

The bioavailability, taste masking, and release profile of new generations of ODTs have been improved. The variety of medicinal uses for ODTs was further expanded thanks to the high load of APIs and exceptionally poor taste-masking medicines that were produced. Rapidly dispersing microgranules, a direct compression blend, and an external tablet lubrication technique are some of the innovative technologies used in ODTs. With a friability test of less than 0.5 percent, the new generation may be packaged in bottles or blister packs and has outstanding physical strength to handle transit. other characteristics like disintegration qualities and mouth feel. They were able to achieve 15 to 30 seconds of breakdown and deliver an API granule and carrier mixture that is smoothly flavoured and simple to swallow. ODT's technology and micro encapsulation have successfully collaborated to create a mask that can withstand extremely bitter APIs and be used in both soluble and poorly soluble compounds as well as high dose products. The medication particles are entirely encapsulated and offer the best flavour masking thanks to the coacervation process. It is immediately applied by uniformly coating polymeric membranes of various thicknesses and porosities with a homogeneous coating over the dry crystals or granules of the medication. This will result in granules with a membrane that serves as both a stabilisation barrier between the API and the tablet excipients and an inert barrier between the API and taste buds, with a size range of 105 to 300 microns. Some of the really bad tasting medications have been taste-masked using this common masking approach. However, there are still some challenges for ODTs such as using polymers as a taste mask to achieve bioequivalence. The polymers may prevent drug release in the gastrointestinal tract and postpone the start of effect. Using a micro encapsulation technique restricts dissolution of the API in the mouth, but allows rapid dissolution in the GI tract, therefore overcoming the bio equivalence obstacle as given in **Figure.**

2.1. Microencapsulation restricts dissolution of API in mouth but allows rapid dissolution in the GI Tract.

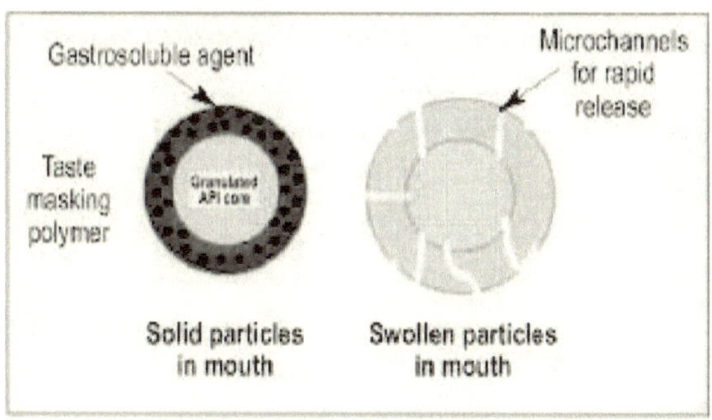

Figure. 2.1 Microencapsulation restricts dissolution of API in mouth but allows rapid dissolution in the GI Tract.

Pharmacokinetics of ODTs

Once a drug is administered in the mouth, it will be absorbed, reach the therapeutic level, and unleash the pharmacological action. Consequently, pace and prolonged absorption are crucial.. The greater disintegration period of conventional dosage forms of tablets will eventually cause a delay in the dissolution release. The disintegration time and dissolution release are significantly faster than ODTs. The mouth is where the absorption begins, followed by the pharynx and oesophagus until the saliva reaches the stomach.

Age, gastrointestinal tract (GI) pH, blood flow through GI tract are some factors that should be taken into consideration when prescribing ODTs especially for old population since they tend to have a decrease in body mass and total body water, which eventually lead to a reduction in volume of distribution (Vd) for water soluble drugs whereas the opposite to lipid soluble drugs, the volume of distribution will be increased. Another factor also for such population is liver volume. The blood flow to the liver will consequently diminish, which will slow down the drug's biotransformation through oxidation, reduction, and hydrolysis. All of these elements will impact renal clearance and the lengthening of half-life.

Alzheimer's disease (AD)

Definition

The type of dementia that is most often recognised is Alzheimer's disease (AD). "Dementia" is a general term used to describe a variety of disorders and conditions that develop when brain nerve cells (called neurons) pass away or lose the ability to function normally. Neuronal degeneration or death causes changes in a person's memory, behaviour, and ability to think clearly. These brain alterations in AD eventually make it difficult for a person to walk and swallow, two basic physical activities. AD is fatal in the end. (Thies *et al.*, 2013).

History

German neurologist and psychiatrist Alois Alzheimer first identified the condition in 1906. (Alzheimer's Association, 2010). Auguste D., 51, was the first person to be diagnosed with the illness. In 1901, her family brought her to Dr. Alzheimer after she underwent identity changes that affected her personality and behaviour. The family claimed memory problems, communication difficulties, and impaired perception. Later, Dr. Alzheimer said that Auguste had a severe form of dementia that manifested in memory, linguistic, and behavioural deficits. (Khachaturian *et al.*, 1996). Dr. Alzheimer noted numerous strange side effects, incorporating trouble with discourse, disturbance, and disarray. Until her death in 1906, he followed her for five years. Following her death, Dr. Alzheimer conducted a post-mortem during which he found spectacular cerebral cortical shrinkage, fatty deposits in the veins, and degenerating brain cells. He discovered neurofibrillary tangles and weak plaques, which must be indicative of AD. (Alzheimer's Drug Discovery Foundation). Alzheimer's disease was first mentioned in medical literature in 1907, and it was given that name in 1910.

Alzheimer's disease Vs dementia and normal aging

The disease of Alzheimer's is frequently confused with normal ageing and dementia. Extreme memory loss, which is a hallmark of AD, is not a sign of normal ageing. Hair, weight, stature, and mass loss can all occur naturally as we age. Skin sensitivity and bone density loss are both possible side effects. Additionally to a declining metabolic rate, hearing and vision impairments may also occur. It is common to experience a minor decline in memory, as seen in slower data review, but Psychological deterioration that interferes with daily life is not a typical part of the ageing process.

(www.webmd.com).

Dementia is characterised by a considerable decline in cognitive abilities that is severe enough to affect social interaction. It may be caused by a number of illnesses that harm brain cells. There are numerous varieties of dementia, each with a unique aetiology and set of signs and symptoms. For instance, vascular dementia is brought on by reduced blood supply to a specific area of the brain following a stroke. Patients with hydrocephalus and Parkinson's disease may also have dementia. The most prevalent type of dementia, AD, is brought on by the accumulation of beta amyloid plaques in the brain.

(www.medterms.com).

Prevalence

According to Alzheimer's disease International, the expected number of dementia sufferers globally in 2013 was 44.4 million. By 2030 and 2050, this number will rise to 75.6 million and 135.5 million, respectively. By 2050, 71% of the population will have dementia, up from the current 62% in emerging nations. China, India, and their other neighbours in south Asia and the western Pacific region are seeing the fastest increases in their elderly populations.

Population ageing is a global phenomenon that highlights the successes of improved social insurance over the past century. The world population now contains a greater proportion of older people since people are living longer and healthier lives. Although instances that start b There are 7.7 million new instances of dementia each year, which indicates that there is always another case somewhere on the earth. There fore the age of 65 are becoming more common, dementia primarily affects older people.

(Dementia statistics).

Pathophysiology of AD

The neurofibrillary tangles (NFTs) in the medial temporal lobe structures and cortical regions of the brain, along with a degeneration of the neurons and synapses, are the hallmark lesions in AD at the microscopic level. Amyloid beta (A) aggregation and deposition with plaque development, hyperphosphorylation with tangle formation, and other mechanisms including inflammatory processes and oxidative stress have all been explored as pathogenic mechanisms underlying these alterations. (Blennow *et al.*, 2006).

Plaque formation

Major cleavage sites for three separate enzymatic activity (-, -, and - secretases) are present in the amyloid precursor protein (APP), which is what causes senile plaque to form. In Figure 2.2, the sequence of A is denoted by a black box within its precursor protein APP. During the processing of APP, A is either liberated from APP by cleavages by - and -secretases or divided by -secretase. The cleavage of APP by -secretase, also known as -site APP cleavage enzyme 1 (BACE1), occurs at the N-terminus of the A domain in the amyloidogenic pathway, producing secreted sAPP (soluble APP fragments) as well as a C-terminal fragment of APP that is 99 amino acids long (C99). The - secretase then further cleaves C99 within its transmembrane domain, resulting in the secretion of the production of the APP intracellular domain and the A peptide. The A peptide has a propensity to clump, and A oligomers are harmful to the brain.

Finally, A-peptides are deposited in the brain as amyloid plaques. The amyloidogenic route is made up of the sequential cleavage of APP by - and -secretase, which results in A. The neurotrophic and neuroprotective sAPP (soluble APP fragments) are produced by cleavage of APP by -secretase within the A peptide domain in the non-amyloidogenic pathway, and because -secretase cleaves inside the A sequence, A is not produced. Following APP cleavage by -secretase, -secretase further cleaves the C-terminal 83 (C83) amino acids comprising fragment of APP, causing the smaller non-amyloidogenic p3 peptide to be secreted and the production of AICD. (Postina, 2008).

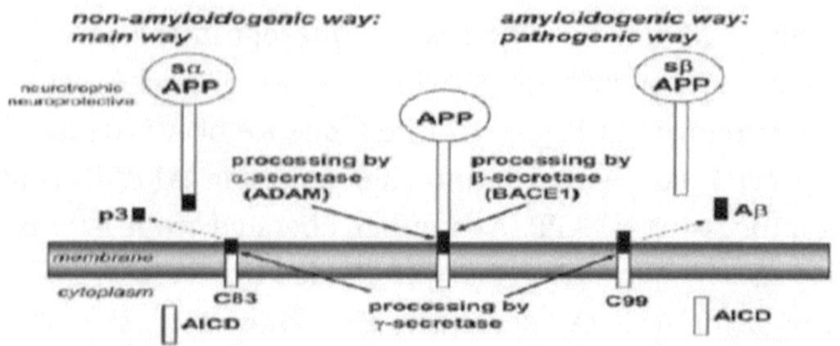

Figure 2.2 Enter CaProteolytic processing of APP via the non-amyloidogenic and the amyption

Neurofibrillary tangles (NFTs)

A was discovered in plaques almost simultaneously with the discovery that tangles were made of abnormally hyperphosphorylated tau (p-tau) protein. Normal axonal protein tau promotes microtubule assembly and stability by interacting with microtubules through its microtubule-binding domains. (**Figure. 2.3**).

The harmony between various kinases and phosphates controls the amount of tau that is phosphorylated. P-tau in AD begins intracellularly and sequesters normal tau and other microtubule-associated proteins. This impairs axonal transport by causing microtubule breakdown and compromises neuronal and synaptic function. In tangles, tau also develops a propensity to aggregate into insoluble fibrils, further impairing neuronal function.

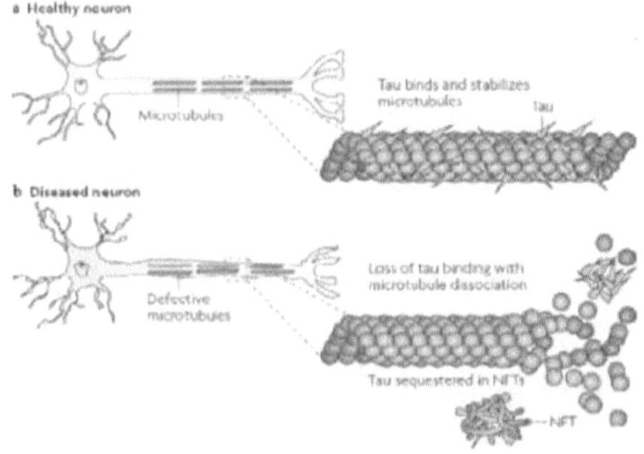

Enter **Figure.2.3** Tau in healthy neurons and in diseased neuronsCaption

Inflammation

The inflammatory hypothesis, whose main idea is a self-perpetuating, progressive inflammation in the brain that results in neurodegeneration, is a popular theory to explain the pathophysiology of AD. There are currently no recognised local initiating inflammatory causes for AD. It has been hypothesised that the pathologic characteristics of AD, such as A1-42 found in senile plaques, p-tau protein found in neurofibrillary tangles, or elements of dying neurons, may cause inflammation. Tumor necrosis factor- (TNF-) and interleukin-1 are thought to be produced by glial cells in response to these pathologic alterations. (IL-1β) (**Figure . 2.4**).

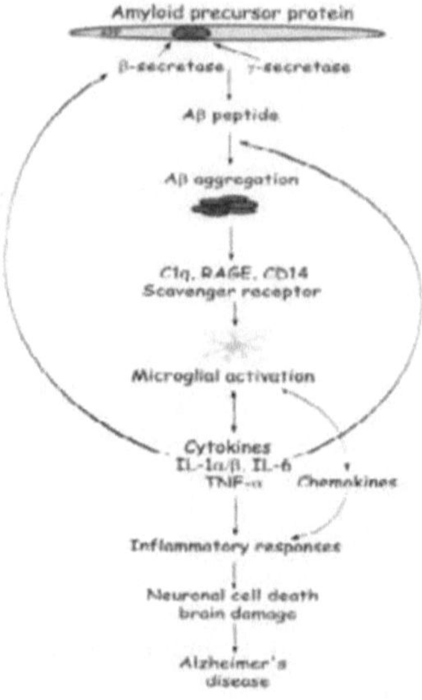

Figure. 2.4 Inflammatory pathway in Alzheimer's disease (Kamer *et al.*, 2008)

Elevated pro-inflammatory cytokines may subsequently induce the production of more A-42, p-tau, and pro-inflammatory chemicals by glial cells through paracrine and/or autocrine mechanisms. As a result, a vicious cycle is created in which inflammatory mediators stimulate glial cells while also triggering biochemical pathways that result in neurodegeneration. This model has a lot of supporting data. Senile plaques are characterised by reactive astrocytes, activated microglial cells, and immunological responses with TNF- and IL-1-antibodies. TNF-α and IL-1β are capable of stimulating the synthesis of $A\beta_{42}$ and the p-tau, and $A\beta_{42}$ and p-tau can stimulate the production of

TNF-α and IL-1β by glial cells (Kamer *et al.*, 2008).

Treatment of Alzheimer's disease

There is currently no treatment for Alzheimer's disease (AD), however a number of drugs have been shown to slow the illness's course and treat its symptoms. When treating AD patients, medical professionals separate the symptoms into "cognitive" and "behavioural and psychiatric" groups. This makes it possible to administer treatment according to the manifestations being experienced. Cognitive disorders have an impact on viewpoints, dialect, memory, and judgement. Behavioural side effects modify a persisting activities and feelings (www.alz.org).

Treatment for cognitive symptoms

Modifying the effect of chemical messengers in the brain is one aspect of treating cognitive disorders. For this reason, two different types of medicine have received FDA approval.

The most common type is a cholinesterase inhibitor, which messes with the enzyme in control of acetylcholine breakdown in the brain.

A crucial neurotransmitter involved in memory and learning is acetylcholine. Acetylcholine focus slightly decreases with age, resulting in sporadic forgetfulness. But in AD, the focus can be reduced by up to 90%, leading to a significant decline in memory and behaviour. These drugs have the purpose of improving nerve cell communication, which increases the amount of acetylcholine in the body. Three cholinesterase inhibitors—donepezil, galantamine, and rivastigmine—are commonly recommended.

Memantine is a drug that has been licenced for the treatment of AD in addition to cholinesterase inhibitors. Memantine controls how glutamate behaves in the brain.

An excitatory neurotransmitter involved in memory and learning is glutamate. (Riedel *et al.*, 2003). Excitotoxicity, the term used to describe the neuronal degeneration seen in AD, may be caused by glutamate overstimulation of neurons. (Reisberg *et al.*, 2003). N-methyl-D-aspartate (NMDA) receptors are found on the surface of brain cells and are linked to glutamate. Memantine prevents the NMDA receptors from functioning, protecting the nerves from unneeded glutamate incitation. (Reisberg *et al.*, 2003). Memantine can, incidentally, delay the deterioration of cognitive symptoms and is suggested for the treatment of moderate to severe AD. List of approved drugs for treating Alzheimer's was given in **Table 2.1**

Drug Name	Condition	Action	Dose
Donepezil Brand Name: Aricept	Mild to severe AD	Prevents the breakdown of acetylcholine (ACh) by inhibiting the action of acetyl cholinesterase and treats cognitive symptoms of AD	5 mg taken once per day Over time, may increase to 10 mg daily
Galantamine Brand Name: Razadyne	Mild to moderate AD	Prevents the breakdown of acetylcholine and stimulates receptors to release excess ACh and treats cognitive symptoms of AD	4 mg taken twice daily Over time, may increase to a maximum of 24 mg per day
Rivastigmine Brand Name: Exelon	Mild to moderate AD Also used to treat dementia from Parkinson's disease	Prevents the breakdown of acetylcholine by inhibiting the enzymes that degrade ACh and treats cognitive symptoms of AD	1.5 mg taken twice per day Over time, may increase to a maximum of 12 mg per day
Memantine Brand Name: Namenda	Moderate to severe AD	Blocks glutamatergic (NMDA) receptors and regulates the action of glutamate and treats cognitive symptoms of AD	5 mg taken once per day Over time, may increase to a maximum of 10 mg per day

Treatment for behavioral and psychiatric symptoms

In addition to severe behavioural and mental symptoms, AD can cause cognitive and functional decline. Unease, agitation, fomentation, delusions, and hallucinations are among these symptoms. Possible treatment strategies include non-medicate mediations and solutions to treat the manifestations being exhibited. Changing nature to remove obstacles and provide security is a potent non-medication strategy. (Alzheimer's infection fact sheet). Another option is to look into possible interactions between long-term medications that can have detrimental effects on behaviour or mental health. Medication may be needed if these treatments are ineffective in alleviating the symptoms. Depending on the side effects, other medications could be chosen. An energizer, such as Prozac or Zoloft, can be recommended, for example, if the patient is feeling dejected. Antipsychotics and anxiolytics may be taken to lessen mental trips and tension, respectively (Alzheimer's disease fact sheet).

Treatment for behavioral and psychiatric symptoms

In addition to severe behavioural and mental symptoms, AD can cause cognitive and functional decline. Unease, agitation, fomentation, delusions, and hallucinations are among these symptoms. Possible treatment strategies include non-medicate mediations and solutions to treat the manifestations being exhibited. Changing nature to remove obstacles and provide security is a potent non-medication strategy. (Alzheimer's infection fact sheet). Another option is to look into possible interactions between long-term medications that can have detrimental effects on behaviour or mental health. Medication may be needed if these treatments are ineffective in alleviating the symptoms. Depending on the side effects, other medications could be chosen. An energizer, such as Prozac or Zoloft, can be recommended, for example, if the patient is feeling dejected. Antipsychotics and anxiolytics may be taken to lessen mental trips and tension, respectively (Alzheimer's disease fact sheet).

CHAPTER THREE

PLAN OF WORK

Phase I: Characterization of pure drug
    Drug-Excipient compatability study
    Isothermal stress testing (IST)
    Assessment of physical instability
    Assessment of chemical instability
    Fourier transform infra red spectroscopy (FTIR)
    Differential scanning calorimetry (DSC)

Phase II: Analytical Hierarchy Process (AHP)

Selection of a suitable method for the preparation of orodispersible tablets using decision making tool (Analytical Hierarchy Process)

Phase III: Formulation

To create orodispersible tablets for the chosen medications (galantamine HBr, memantine HCl, and donepezil HCl) using a suitable approach by chosen method using three different approaches: superdisintegrant addition, effervescence, and sublimation, in addition to combined approaches in accordance with the formulae to be prepared..

Phase IV: Evaluation studies

Preformulation studies should be carried out to determine the flow characteristics of produced granules, such as bulk density, tapped density compressibility index, hausner's ratio, and angle of repose.

To perform physico-chemical assessment tests on the generated formulations, including weight variation, thickness, hardness, friability, weight variation, wetting time, disintegration test, and homogeneity of drug content.

To achieve rapid drug dissolution and absorption that could result in a rapid onset of action for a subset of drugs (Galantamine HBr, Memantine HCl, and Donepezil HCl), an in vitro release study using the USP Dissolution Testing Apparatus II should be conducted, and the release rate should be measured using HPLC.

The kinetics of drug release will be examined by graphing the in vitro release data using different kinetics models.

The optimal formula should be chosen and optimised based on the precompression, postcompression, and in vitro drug release study outcomes. The results were subjected to ANOVA in order to choose and optimise the optimal formulation based on the results above.

Phase V: *In vivo* bioavailability study

Phase VI: Comparative study

Wistar rats should be used as the animal model for the bioavailability study in order to analyse the bioavailability parameters of the produced tablets of Galantamine HBr, Memantine HCl, and Donepezil HCl.

To carry out comparative study for the formulated three different drugs of same class.

It is important to compare the findings of all the studies. Comparisons should be made, in particular, between each drug's optimal formulation and its marketed produ

Phase VII: Stability studies

According to ICH standards, stability studies on the improved formulas of three pharmaceuticals (Galantamine HBr, Memantine HCl, and Donepezil HCl) are to be carried out for six months at a temperature of 40°C/2°C and a relative humidity of 75% RH/5%.

CHAPTER FOUR

MATERIALS & METHODS

List of Chemicals used

The chemicals used in this research work were obtained from the commercial sources (table1) and used without any further purification. They were of analytical reagent grade and used as such.

S.No. Chemical Manufacturer

1. Mannitol Merck (India) Ltd (Mumbai, India)
2. Colloidal silicon dioxide Sigma-Aldrich (Bangalore, India)
3. Magnesium stearate Sigma-Aldrich (Bangalore, India)
4. Purified talc Sigma-Aldrich (Bangalore, India)
5. Aspartame Sigma-Aldrich (Bangalore, India)
6. Sodium chloride Merck (India) Ltd (Mumbai, India)
7. Sodium Hydroxide Merck (India) Ltd (Mumbai, India)
8. Water for HPLC Merck (India) Ltd (Mumbai, India)
9. Disodium hydrogen phosphate Sigma-Aldrich (Bangalore, India)
10. Potassium Dihydrogen ortho phosphate Sigma-Aldrich (Bangalore, India)

11. Acetonitrile Merck (India) Ltd (Mumbai, India)
12. Ammonium acetate Merck (India) Ltd (Mumbai, India)
13. Potassium bromide Merck (India) Ltd (Mumbai, India)
14. Hydrochloric acid Merck (India) Ltd (Mumbai, India)
15. Aspartame Sigma-Aldrich (Bangalore, India)
16. Sodium chloride Merck (India) Ltd (Mumbai, India)
17. Sodium Hydroxide Merck (India) Ltd (Mumbai, India)
18. Water for HPLC Merck (India) Ltd (Mumbai, India)
19. Disodium hydrogen phosphate Sigma-Aldrich (Bangalore, India)
20. Potassium Sigma-Aldrich (Bangalore, India)
21. Dihydrogen ortho phosphate Sigma-Aldrich (Bangalore, India)
22. Acetonitrile Merck (India) Ltd (Mumbai, India)
23. Ammonium acetate Merck (India) Ltd (Mumbai, India)
24. Potassium bromide Merck (India) Ltd (Mumbai, India)
25. Hydrochloric acid Merck (India) Ltd (Mumbai, India)

List of Instruments used

The instruments used in this research work were listed in table 2 along with model number and manufacturer information.

S.No. Instruments Model & Manufacturer

1. Differential Scanning Calorimetry DSC- 60, Shimadzu, Japan
2. FT-IR Spectrometer Nicolet iS5, Thermo Scientific
3. Water Purification Plant Milli-Q Academic, Milli-Pore.
4. Vernier calliper Dalian Mingfeng Machinery Co., Ltd
5. Hardness tester Monsanto.
6. Tablet Friabilater Roche friabilator (ERWEKA).
7. HPLC Shimadzu, Japan
8. Mechanical Stirrer RQT-124A, Remi.

9. Digital pH meter Eutech Instruments
10. Disintegration Test Apparatus H-7500, Hitachi.
11. Dissolution Test Apparatus USP Type II Electrolab
12. Centrifuge C-24, Remi.
13. Tablet punching machine 10 stations, Erweka, Germany

Drug Profile
Galantamine hydrobromide Description

A benzazepine derived from norbelladine. It is found in galanthus and other amaryllidaceae. Galantamine is a cholinesterase inhibitor that has been used to reverse the muscular effects of gallamine triethiodide and tubocurarine, and has been studied as a treatment for Alzheimer's disease and other central nervous system disorders. Galantamine, a reversible, competitive acetylcholinesterase inhibitor, is present in galantamine hydrobromide extended-release capsules and galantamine tablets USP.

Molecular Formula : $C_{17}H_{22}NO_3Br$

Molecular Weight : 368.3 g/mol

Chemical Name :(4aS,8aR)-3-methoxy-11-methyl-5,6,9,10,11,12-hexahydro-4aH-benzo[2,3] benzofuro[4,3-cd]azepin-6- ol hydrobromide

Functional category : Treatment of Alzheimer's disease

Description : white to almost white powder

Solubility : sparingly soluble in water, freely soluble in alcohol, acetone, and chloroform; less soluble in benzene

Melting point : 256 °C

Storage : Store at -20° C

Half life : 7 hours

Mechanism of Action

It has been noted that acetylcholine-producing neurons degrade in the brains of Alzheimer's disease (AD) patients, despite the fact that the cause of cognitive impairment in AD is not entirely known. The degree of cognitive impairment and the density of amyloid plaques have been associated with this cholinergic decline. (a neuropathological hallmark of Alzheimer's disease).

Acetylcholinesterase is competitively and irreversibly inhibited by galantamine, a tertiary alkaloid. Galantamine is thought to exercise its therapeutic effects via boosting cholinergic activity, while its exact mode of action is uncertain. This is done by reversibly inhibiting cholinesterase's hydrolysis of acetylcholine, which raises the concentration of the neurotransmitter. If this mechanism is accurate, the impact of galantamine may diminish as the disease process progresses and fewer functionally intact cholinergic neurons are left. There is no evidence that galantamine alters the course of the underlying dementing process.

Pharmacokinetics

The pharmacokinetics of galantamine are linear over a dose range of 8 to 32 mg/day.

Absorption and Distribution

Galantamine takes about an hour to absorb and reach its maximal concentration. About 90% of galantamine is absolutely bioavailable. The oral solution formulation's bioavailability was the same as that of the tablet formulation. Galantamine's AUC was unaffected by food, but when it was given together with food, the Cmax was reduced by 25% and the Tmax was delayed by 1.5 hours. Galantaminc's typical distribution volume is 175L. At therapeutically relevant dosages, galantamine has an 18% plasma protein binding. Galantamine is mostly found in blood cells (52.7%) in whole blood. Galantamine has a 1.2 blood to plasma concentration ratio.

Metabolism and Elimination

Galantamine is converted to glucuronidated excretion in the urine by hepatic cytochrome P450 enzymes. Galantamine's oral bioavailability is moderately increased by inhibitors of both of the primary cytochrome P450 isoenzymes involved in its metabolism, cytochrome CYP2D6 and CYP3A4, according to in vitro investigations. O-demethylation was more prevalent in CYP2D6 extensive metabolizers compared to poor metabolizers. However, unaltered galantamine and its glucuronide accounted for the majority of the sample radioactivity in plasma from both poor and extensive metabolizers.

Pharmacodynamics

Galantamine is a reversible cholinesterase inhibitor and a parasympathomimetic. It is recommended for the treatment of mild to moderate Alzheimer's-related dementia. A lack of acetylcholine caused by the selective death of cholinergic neurons in the cerebral cortex, nucleus basalis, and hippocampus is an early pathophysiological hallmark of Alzheimer's disease that is linked to memory loss and cognitive difficulties. Galantamine is thought to improve cholinergic function in order to have its therapeutic effects. This is done by reversibly inhibiting acetylcholinesterase's hydrolysis of acetylcholine to increase the amount of acetylcholine in the system. Galantamine's impact might diminish as the condition worsens and fewer functionally intact cholinergic neurons remain if this suggested mode of action is accurate. There is no proof that galantamine affects the dementing process' fundamental path.

Dosage

Galantamine pills should first be taken at a dose of 4 mg twice daily (8 mg/day). After a minimum of 4 weeks, the dosage should be increased to the initial maintenance dosage of 8 mg twice daily (16 mg/day). After at least four weeks at 8 mg twice a day, a further increase to 12 mg twice a day (24 mg/day) should be tried. (16 mg/day).

Adverse drug reactions

Serious adverse reactions are discussed in more detail in the following sections of the labeling:

Serious skin reactions

Deaths in subjects with mild cognitive impairment (MCI)

Memantine hydrochloride Description

Memantine is a derivative of amantadine with low to moderate NMDA receptor affinity. It is a noncompetitive NMDA receptor antagonist that binds cation channels controlled by NMDA receptors. It counteracts the effects of excess glutamate, which can cause neuronal dysfunction. Although it is being researched for the treatment of Alzheimer's disease, there is no clinical evidence to suggest that it can stop or halt the illness's progression.

The tablets are available as 5 mg, 10 mg or 20 mg of memantine hydrochloride. The oral solution contains 2 mg of memantine hydrochloride per ml.

Structural Formula

Molecular Formula : $C_{12}H_{22}ClN$

Molecular Weight : 215.1 g/mol

Chemical Name : 1-Amino-3,5-dimethyladamantane. HCl **Functional category :** Treatment of Alzheimer's disease

Description : Fine white to off-white powder

Solubility : freely soluble in ethanol and methanol, soluble in water, sparingly soluble in chloroform, and almost insoluble in acetone and insoluble in isopropanol.

Melting point : 258 °C

Storage : Store at room temperature

Half life : 60 to 100 hours

Mechanism of Action

Memantine works by preferentially interacting with NMDA receptor-operated cation channels to inhibit their function through noncompetitive NMDA receptor antagonism. Dementia sufferers have persistently higher levels of glutamate in their brains, which is enough to prevent the voltage-dependent inhibition of NMDA receptors by Mg2+ ions and enable a steady flow of Ca2+ ions into cells, which ultimately leads to neuronal death. According to studies, memantine binds to the NMDA receptor more tightly than Mg2+ ions, thereby blocking the sustained influx of Ca2+ ions while preserving the brief physiological activation of the channels caused by larger quantities of synaptically released glutamate. Memantine thus offers defence against persistently high glutamate levels. Memantine also contains adverse decreased antagonistic activity at the nicotinic acetylcholine receptor and activity at the type 3 serotonergic (5-HT3) receptor with potencies comparable to those at the NMDA receptor. GABA, benzodiazepines, dopamine, adrenergic, histamine, or glycine receptors are not influenced by this medication, nor are voltage-dependent calcium, sodium, or potassium channels.

Pharmacokinetics

Absorption

Memantine is readily absorbed after oral treatment, reaching peak concentrations in 3 to 7 hours. Over the therapeutic dose range, the pharmacokinetics of memantine are linear. Food has no impact on how well memantine is absorbed..

Distribution

The mean volume of distribution of memantine is 9-11 L/kg and the plasma protein binding is low (45%).

Metabolism

Memantine is partially metabolised in the liver. The metabolism of memantine does not significantly involve the hepatic microsomal CYP450 enzyme system.

Elimination

Memantine is excreted predominantly (about 48%) unchanged in urine and has a terminal elimination half-life of about 60-80 hours. The remaining material is predominantly transformed into the N-glucuronide conjugate, 6-hydroxy memantine, and 1-nitroso-deaminated memantine, three polar metabolites with limited NMDA receptor antagonistic action. The parent medication and the N-glucuronide conjugate are excreted together in amounts totaling 74% of the administered dose. Active tubular secretion, which is controlled by pH-dependent tubular reabsorption, is a component of renal clearance.

Pharmacodynamics

An NMDA receptor antagonist called memantine, an amantadine derivative, is used to treat Alzheimer's disease. It differs from conventional Alzheimer's disease treatments in that it works on glutamatergic neurotransmission rather than cholinergic neurotransmission. There is some proof that the neuronal excitotoxicity caused by glutamatergic neurotransmission failure, which causes Alzheimer's disease, is related to its aetiology. As a result, given the ineffectiveness of current medications that target the cholinergic system, targeting the glutamatergic system, specifically NMDA receptors, was a fresh approach to treatment. Memantine improves cognition, mood, behaviour, and the capacity to carry out daily tasks, according to a systematic analysis of randomised controlled studies. There is no proof that memantine helps patients with Alzheimer's disease avoid or slow neurodegeneration.

Dosage

NAMENDA is best taken once daily at a dose of 5 mg (2.5 mL). The dosage should be raised by 5 mg increments, going from 5 mg to 10 mg (2.5 mL twice daily), 15 mg (2.5 mL and 5 mL as separate doses), and 20 mg (2.5 mL and 10 mL as one dose) (5 mL twice daily). The One week minimum time between dose increases is advised. 20 mg/day is the dosage that controlled clinical trials have demonstrated to be effective (5 mL twice daily).

Adverse drug reactions

Confusion, drowsiness, headaches, sleeplessness, agitation, and/or hallucinations are typical adverse medication reactions (1% of patients). Vomiting, anxiety, hypertonia, cystitis, and enhanced libido are less frequent side effects. It has been claimed to cause reversible neurological damage in people with multiple sclerosis, which forced the suspension of a clinical trial that was in progress. Extrapyramidal side effects (such as dystonic responses, etc.) are extremely rare but might happen, especially in younger people.

Donepezil hydrochloride Description

A centrally acting reversible acetyl cholinesterase inhibitor is donepezil (Aricept). Its primary medicinal application is raising cortical acetylcholine to treat Alzheimer's disease. The therapeutic effect of donepezil is thought to be achieved by improving cholinergic function. This is done by reversibly inhibiting acetylcholinesterase's breakdown of acetylcholine to raise its levels. If the suggested mode of action is accurate, donepezil's effects may diminish as the disease process worsens and fewer functionally intact cholinergic neurons remain. Lewy body dementia and vascular dementia are two more cognitive illnesses for which donepezil has been investigated, although these uses are not yet permitted. Additionally, patients with mild cognitive impairment, schizophrenia, and attention deficit disorder have been investigated with donepezil. disorder, cognitive impairment following a cardiac bypass. Down syndrome and multiple sclerosis both cause cognitive impairment.

Structural Formula

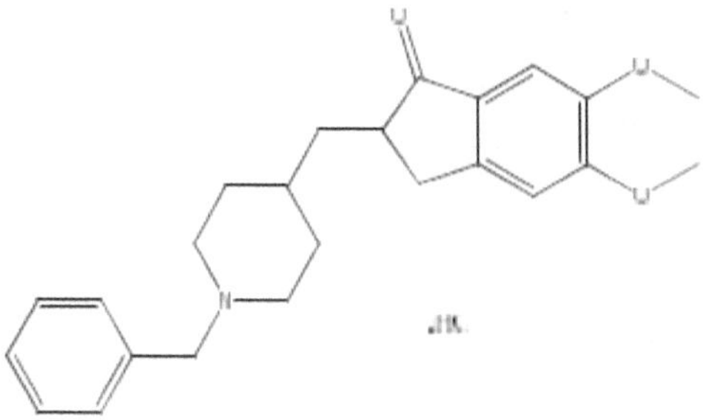

Molecular Formula : $C_{24}H_{30}ClNO_3$

Molecular Weight : 415.9 g/mol

Chemical   Name   :
2-[(1-benzylpiperidin-4-yl)methyl]-5,6-dimethoxy
-2,3-dihydro-1H-inden-1-one

Functional category : Treatment of Alzheimer's disease

Description : White to off-white or slightly yellow crystalline powder

Solubility : freely soluble in chloroform, dichloromethane and in methanol, soluble in water, sparingly soluble in ethanol, n-butanol and in acetonitrile and very slightly soluble in acetone.

Melting point : 206 °C

Storage : Store at -20° C

Half life : 70 hours

Mechanism of Action

In patients with Alzheimer's disease, donepezil's exact mode of action is not entirely understood. It is undeniable that Alzheimer's disease results in a significant loss of the cholinergic system's components, and it is widely acknowledged that the disease's symptoms are connected to this cholinergic deficit, notably in the cerebral cortex and other parts of the brain. It has been highlighted that the hippocampus formation is crucial for controlling activities such as learning, memory, and attention. The level of cognitive impairment has been observed to correspond with the extent of cholinergic neuron loss in the central nervous system (CNS). The cholinesterases are bound and reversibly inactivated by donepezil, which prevents the hydrolysis of acetylcholine. Acetylcholine concentrations at cholinergic synapses rise as a result of this.

Pharmacokinetics

Absorption

T_{max} for the 10 and 23 mg tablets is approximately 3 and 8 h, respectively. C_{max} is almost 2–fold higher for the 23 mg tablet compared with the 10 mg tablet. Steady state is reached in 15 days.

Distribution

Volume of distribution is 12 to 16 L/kg (at steady state). Approximately 96% protein bound (75% to albumin and 21% alpha-1 acid glycoprotein)

Metabolism

Metabolized by CYP2D6 and CYP3A4, and undergoes glucuronidation to 4 major metabolites (2 active) and several minor metabolites.

Elimination

The elimination half-life is approximately 70 h. Cl is 0.13 to 0.19 L/h/kg. Approximately 57% recovered in urine and 15% in feces; approximately 17% of dose is recovered unchanged in urine.

Pharmacodynamics

A centrally acting, reversible acetyl cholinesterase inhibitor is donepezil. Its primary medicinal application is raising cortical acetylcholine to treat Alzheimer's disease. A lack of acetylcholine as a result of the selective loss of cholinergic neurons in the cerebral cortex, nucleus basalis, and hippocampus is an early pathophysiological hallmark of Alzheimer's disease that is linked to memory loss and cognitive difficulties.

It is hypothesised that donepezil improves cholinergic activity in order to have a therapeutic effect. This is done by reversibly inhibiting acetylcholinesterase's breakdown of acetylcholine to raise its levels. If the suggested mode of action is accurate, donepezil's impact might diminish as the disease worsens and fewer functionally intact cholinergic neurons are left. There is no proof that donepezil affects the underlying dementing process' course.

Dosage

Before commencing on ARICEPT 23 mg/day, patients should be on ARICEPT 10 mg/day for at least 3 months. The starting dose of ARICEPT is 5 mg/day and can be increased to 10 mg/day after 4-6 weeks. Please take ARICEPT exactly as directed by your physician.

Adverse effects

Nausea, diarrhoea, and vomiting were the most frequent side effects in clinical studies that led to withdrawal. Anorexia, cramping in the muscles, and trouble sleeping were further adverse effects. Compared to 10 mg or lower levels, patients receiving the 23 mg dose experienced the majority of the adverse events. With time, side symptoms diminished.

METHODS

Characterization of pure drug

Reliable sources were used to procure the medications and excipients for the research project. To authenticate these medications and excipients, a Fourier Transform Infrared (FTIR) Spectrophotometer was used to determine their functional groups and bonds.

Drug Excipient compatibility study

Incompatible drug excipient combinations may interact, which causes either chemical or physical instability. Physical instability describes changes in a drug's properties that don't entail the development or breaking of chemical bonds.alterations in the organoleptic criteria, such as look, form, etc., which can be used to identify changes in the drug structure Chemical instability describes modifications to the drug's chemical structure that cause drug breakdown, a decrease in drug content, and the production of additional molecules such degradation products. Instability on a physical or chemical level could raise safety issues. Consequently, it is essential to conduct a complete drug/drug excipient compatibility research

Isothermal stress testing (IST) (Liltorp okay et al., 2011; Moorthi C et al., 2013)

The IST method, which involves storing samples with or without moisture at a high temperature, is frequently used to evaluate the compatibility of medicine and drug excipient. Then, using FTIR, structural alterations and organoleptic characteristics were evaluated to identify the physical instability. (Liltorp *et al*, 2011)

Sample preparation

Pure drugs and excipients were weighed as per table 5.3 to table 5.5. In order to integrate the mixtures, each combination was carefully ground in a clean glass mortar. Individual medications, individual excipients, and prepared blends were put into glass vials with the proper labels. Each vial was then filled with 10 L of extremely pure water (Milli-Q Academic, Milli-Pore), mixed with a glass capillary, and then placed back into the vial. Each vial was carefully sealed and kept in a hot air oven (T26/HAO-L, Technico) for four weeks at 50°C (Moorthi C et al, 2013).

Table 5.3 Samples for drug excipients compatibility studies of Galantamine HBr

Table 5.3 Samples for drug excipients compatibility studies of Galantamine HBr

Sample	Contents		Ratio
1	Galantamine		-
2	Galantamine	+ Crospovidone + Croscarmellose sodium + Sodium starch glycolate	Equal ratio
3	Galantamine	+ Sodiumbicarbonate + citric acid	Equal ratio
4	Galantamine	+ Camphor	Equal ratio

Table 5.4 Samples for drug excipients compatibility studies of Memantine HCl

Sample	Contents		Ratio
1	Memantine		-
2	Memantine	+ Crospovidone + Croscarmellose sodium + Sodium starch glycolate	Equal ratio
3	Memantine	+ Sodiumbicarbonate + citric acid	Equal ratio
4	Memantine	+ Camphor	Equal ratio

Table 5.5 Samples for drug excipients compatibility studies of Donepezil HCl

Sample	Contents		Ratio
1	Donepezil		-
2	Donepezil	+ Crospovidone + Croscarmellose sodium + Sodium starch glycolate	Equal ratio
3	Donepezil	+ Sodiumbicarbonate + citric acid	Equal ratio
4	Donepezil	+ Camphor	Equal ratio

Assessment of physical instability

Organoleptic characteristics, such as colour and texture, were initially evaluated and recorded for all the samples in order to determine the physical instability. Each sample's colour and texture were assessed visually at the end of the first, second, third, and fourth weeks and compared to the colour and texture at the beginning of the study.

Assessment of chemical instability

At the end of 4th week, samples were used to record the FTIR spectrum and analysed for DSC.

Fourier transform infra red spectroscopy (FTIR)

On an FTIR spectrophotometer, the IR spectra of pure drugs and combinations of drugs and their excipients were captured. 400 mg of dry potassium bromide was used to combine the samples, which were subsequently compressed into transparent discs at a pressure of 10.000–15.000 psi. The scanning range for the IR spectra was 500-4000 cm-1 with a resolution of 4 cm-1. (Shirwaikar R *et al*, 2007)

Differential scanning calorimetry (DSC)

To counteract the oxidative and pyrolytic effects, samples of pure Galantamine HBr, Memantine HCl, Donepezil HCl, and their physical mixtures with various excipients were heated in the DSC instrument (Shimadzu, Japan) in an atmosphere of nitrogen while being hermetically sealed in flat-bottomed aluminium pans. In a temperature range of 25 to 300 0C, the heating rate was 50C/min. Records of the DSC thermograms were made.

Analytical Hierarchy Process (AHP)

Selection of a suitable method for the preparation of orodispersible tablets using decision making tool (Manikandan Mahalingam *et al*, 2015 and Velmurugan R, *et al 2011*)

There are several ways to make orodispersible tablets; in this article, we've focused on some of the most popular ones, including freeze drying, spray drying, and direct compression. However, choosing the right approach was crucial because doing so could waste time, money, and other resources on research as well as being unsuitable.

As a result, an analytical hierarchy process (AHP)-based decision-making tool was employed in the choice of an appropriate technique for producing orodispersible tablets. Dr. Thomas L. Saaty created the AHP, a multi-criteria decision-making tool, in the 1970s. It has been effectively used in numerous disciplines, including marketing, finance, education, public policy, economics, medical, and sports, to determine the best course of action.

Therefore, a decision-making tool based on the analytical hierarchy process (AHP) was used to select the best method for creating orodispersible tablets. The AHP is a multi-criteria decision-making technique that was developed in the 1970s by Dr. Thomas L. Saaty. To choose the optimum course of action, it has been successfully applied in a variety of fields, including marketing, finance, education, public policy, economics, medicine, and sports.

AHP Process

As a first step to make a decision in an organized way a hierarchy model was developed with three levels.

Two main criteria were placed in the second level that is process output and cost.

The goal was placed in the first level. The goal of this AHP exercise is the selection of a suitable method for the preparation of orodispersible tablets.

Three potential methods (Table 5.6) were placed in the third level.

To ascertain the rank for the methods, all three methods were compared with each other for each criterion.

Table 5.6 Potential methods for the preparation of Orodispersible tablets

Consistency ratio (CR) was calculated for the pair wise comparison matrix as follows [CR=CI/RI], where CI is consistency index and calculated as CI = $(\lambda_{max}-n)$ /(n-1) and RI is a random index (consistency index for the n row matrixes of randomly generated comparisons in pairs (Table 5.8).

Table 5.7 Saaty's scale

Importance	Weights	
	i^{th} Vs j^{th}	j^{th} Vs i^{th}
Equally important	1	1
Equally to moderately more important	2	½
Moderately more important	3	1/3
Moderately to strongly more important	4	¼
Strongly more important	5	1/5
Strongly to very strongly more important	6	1/6
Very strongly more important	7	1/7
Very strongly to extremely more important	8	1/8
Extremely more important	9	1/9

Random Index														
n	1	2	3	4	5	6	7	8	9	10	11	12	13	14	15
RI	0,00	0,00	0,52	0,89	1,11	1,25	1,35	1,40	1,45	1,49	1,51	1,54	1,56	1,57	1,58

Formulation of orodispersible tablets

Formulation of Galanatamine hydrobromide ODTs

In accordance with the provided formulae, orodispersible tablets of a few medications were made by the direct compression method utilising three separate procedures: superdisintegrant addition, effervescence, and sublimation, as well as combined approaches. Galantamine HBr orodispersible tablets contain 4 mg of the active ingredient. Total weight of the tablet 100 mg were prepared for all the formulations. In all formulations lactose monohydrate and mannitol were used as diluents. For tablets prepared by sublimationapproach using camphor as a sublimating agent. Citric acid and sodium bicarbonate were employed to produce tablets using the effervescence method. Crospovidone, Croscarmellose sodium, and sodium starch glycolate were employed as superdisintegrants for tablets made using the superdisinterant technique. Prior to mixing, the precise weight of the prescribed amount of the medicine and the other excipients was passed through a 40 # screen. Individual pieces of magnesium stearate were run through #60 mesh. Magnesium stearate was utilised to lubricate the mixture.

The obtained powder mixture was compressed using an 8 mm flat surface punch on a single punch tablet machine (Erweka, Germany) to create tablets. (Nayak *et al*, 2004). The compression force was altered to produce tablets with hardness within the orodispersible tablet pharmacopoeial range (2-4 kg/cm3). All formulations began by carefully combining the weighed amounts of medication and lactose before adding the remaining excipients to load the drug onto the surface of water soluble carriers. Galantamine HBr formulations came in twelve different varieties.

Formulation of Memantine hydrochloride ODTs

In accordance with the provided formulae, orodispersible tablets of memantine hydrochloride were made utilising the direct compression method and three distinct approaches: superdisintegrant addition, effervescence, and sublimation, as well as combined approaches. Memantine HCl orally disintegrating pills provide 5 mg of the active ingredient.

For each formulation, 100 mg of tablet weight total was manufactured. Mannitol and lactose monohydrate were both employed as diluents in all formulations. pertaining to tablets made utilising the sublimation method using camphor as the sublimating ingredient. For effervescently prepared tablets approach, sodium bicarbonate and citric acid were used. Crospovidone, Croscarmellose sodium, and sodium starch glycolate were employed as superdisintegrants for tablets made using the superdisinterant technique. Prior to mixing, the precise weight of the prescribed amount of the medicine and the other excipients was passed through a 40 # screen. Individual pieces of magnesium stearate were run through #60 mesh. Magnesium stearate was utilised to lubricate the mixture.

The obtained powder mixture was compressed using an 8 mm flat surface punch on a single punch tablet machine (Erweka, Germany) to create tablets (Nayak and Gopalkumar, 2004). The compression force was altered to produce tablets with hardness within the orodispersible tablet pharmacopoeial range (2-4 kg/cm3). All formulations began by carefully combining the weighed amounts of medication and lactose before adding the remaining excipients to load the drug onto the surface of water soluble carriers. For memantine HCl, twelve formulations were created.

Formulation of Donepezil hydrochloride ODTs

Utilizing the formulae provided, three alternative approaches—Superdisintegrant addition, effervescence, and sublimation—as well as combined approaches—were used to create orodispersible tablets of chosen medications using the direct compression method. Donepezil HCl orodispersible tablets contain 5 mg of the active ingredient. For each formulation, 100 mg of tablet weight total was manufactured. In all formulations lactose monohydrate and mannitol were used as diluents. For tablets prepared by sublimation approach using camphor as a sublimating agent (Gohel et al., 2004). For tablets prepared by the effervescence approach, sodium bicarbonate and citric acid were used. For tablets prepared by superdisinterant approach Crospovidone, Croscarmellose sodium and sodium starch glycolate were used as superdisintegrants. Prior to mixing, the precise weight of the prescribed amount of the medicine and the other excipients was passed through a 40 # screen. Individual pieces of magnesium stearate were run through #60 mesh. Magnesium stearate was utilised to lubricate the mixture.

The resulting powder mixture was compressed into tablets using single punch tablet machine (Erweka, Germany) using 8 mm flat surface punches (Nayak and Gopalkumar, 2004).

The compression force was altered to produce tablets with hardness within the orodispersible tablet pharmacopoeial range (2-4 kg/cm3). All formulations began by carefully combining the weighed amounts of medication and lactose before adding the remaining excipients to load the drug onto the surface of water soluble carriers. For Donepezil HCl, twelve formulations were developed.

Ingredients weight were mentioned in mg

Characterization of Blend

Micromeritic Properties

Bulk Density and Tapped Density

The blend's micromeritic characteristics, including as bulk density, tapped density, compressibility index, Hausner's ratio, and angle of repose, were assessed before compression.

A graduated measuring cylinder was filled with a predetermined quantity of granules from each formula that had been previously lightly agitated to break any agglomerates that may have formed. After the initial volume was measured, the cylinder was allowed to drop under its own height at intervals of two seconds onto a hard surface. The tapping continued until there was no longer any difference in the volume. BD and TD were calculated using the following formulas (Shah *et al.*, 1997).

BD = Weight of the powder/volume of the packing

TD = Weight of the powder/tapped volume of the packing

Compressibility Index

The compressibility index of the granules was determined by Carr's compressibility index which was calculated by using the following formula: (Aulton M.E, 1988)

Carr's index (%) = [(TD-BD) ×100]/TD

Hausner's Factor

Hausner found that the ratio DF/DO was related to inter particle friction and, as such, could be used to predict powder flow properties (Manikandan M et al, 2012). It is calculated by using the following formula:

Hausner's Factor = TD/BD

Where,

TD is Tapped bulk density and BD is loose bulk density.

Angle of repose

An effective tableting operation depends on the flow qualities. To ensure effective mixing and respectable weight homogeneity for the compressed tablets, a good flow of the powder or granulation is required. Dry powder may occasionally need to be pregranulated to enhance its flow characteristics. The drug's flowability and granulation should be researched throughout the pre-formulation process, especially if a substantial drug dose is anticipated. The angle between the free surface of the static heap and the horizontal plane can reach a specific maximum value for a given powder when the heap of powder is left to stand with only gravity acting on it. It is usual to use this angle, known as the static angle of repose, to explain the flow properties of powder granulation.

In most pharmaceutical powders and granules, the angle of repose values range from 25-40°, with lower values indicating better flow characteristics (Cooper and Gunn, 1986)

The angle of repose is defined as the maximum angle possible between the surface of a pile of powder or granules and the horizontal plane (Cooper and Gunn, 1986).

Tan = h/r

Where, h and r are the height and radius of the powder cone

Evaluation of Tablets

The formulated tablets were evaluated for the following physicochemical parameters.

Thickness

A tablet's thickness can alter without its weight changing. This is typically caused by variations in the granule densities, compression pressure, and compression speed. It was measured by vernier caliper. (United State Pharmacopoeia 30- National Formulary 25, 2007, 634)

Hardness

Tablets need a specific level of strength to resist breaking while being handled and transported, as well as before being used. The Monsanto Hardness Tester was used to measure it. On six tablets, the test was conducted, and the average was determined. (Banker and Anderson, 1987).

Friability test

Using Friabilator, the tablet's friability was ascertained. It's stated as a percentage (%). The Friabilator was then loaded with twenty tablets after they were first weighed (W1). The Friabilator, which subjects tablets to the combined effects of shock and abrasion in a plastic chamber, was run at 25 rpm for 4 minutes, lowering the tablets at a height of 6 inches with each revolution. (Banker and Anderson, 1987). The tablets were de dusted and weighed again (W_2). The % Friability was then calculated by %.

% friability = (W1 - W2 / W1) × 100

Where,

W1 = weight of tablets before test W2 = weight of tablets after test

Weight variation test

Twenty tablets were chosen at random, and each one was weighed. Calculated tablet weights were compared to the weights of the individual tablets. The weight of the tablet must differ from the average weight by no more than two tablets, or 7.5%, for it to be accepted. (Banker and Anderson, 1987).

Disintegration time

Using distilled water at 370.5 °C and a USP disintegration test instrument, the disintegration time was measured. The period at which there were no more tablet granules on the device' mesh was considered to be the disintegration time. Six pills' claimed time for full disintegration was noted. Standard deviations and the mean disintegration time were computed. (Banker and Anderson, 1987; Khan, 1975).

Wetting time

The internal design of the tablets and the excipient's hydrophilicity have a direct impact on wetting time. The hydrophilicity of the powders affects the water penetration rate into the powder bed, which is related to the pore radius. (Tejvir *et al.*, 2011).

It should be evident that as compression force or porosity decreases, pores enlarge and wetting time lengthens. Wetting time and disintegration time have a linear connection. Therefore, wetting is a crucial phase in the integration process. In a petri dish with a 6ml water capacity and an interior diameter of 6.5 cm, tissue paper that had been folded twice was put inside. The tablet was placed on the paper, and the amount of time it took for the tablet to get fully wet was counted in seconds. The procedure was significantly altered by keeping the water at 37 0C. Wetting-time corresponds to the time taken for the tablet to disintegrate when kept motionless on the tongue.

Content uniformity test

Each batch of twenty tablets was powdered and precisely weighed. With the use of the standard calibration curve, the drug content was calculated. The average of three determinations was used to calculate the mean percent drug content. Powder samples were appropriately diluted after being weighed, and HPLC was used to determine the cumulative drug release. (Meyyanathan, 1998).

Dissolution Studies

Using the USP Dissolution Testing Apparatus II, the release rate of orodispersible tablets of three different medications (Galantamine HBr, Memantine HCl, and Donepezil HCl) was assessed (Electro lab, India). 900 cc of phosphate buffer with a pH of 6.8 was used for the dissolving test, which was run at 50 rpm and a temperature of 37 0.5 °C. The percentage of drug release was calculated using HPLC after the sample of 05 ml was removed at intervals of 02 minutes for up to 20 minutes and replaced with fresh medium to maintain sink condition. (Bhagwati and Hiremath, 2005).

Chromatography analysis condition for Galantamine hydro bromide

On a Phenomenex® C18 analytical column (150mm4.6mm i.d., 5m) coupled with a Phenomenex® C18 guard cadridge (4mm3mm i.d., 5m), chromatographic separations were conducted. To ascertain the amount of galantamine hydrobromide, the mobile phase, which included triethylamine phosphate buffer (PBS, pH 6.0) and methanol (75:25), was pumped at a flow rate of 1.0 mL min-1.

Chromatography analysis condition for Memantine hydrochloride

On a Phenomenex® C18 analytical column (150mm4.6mm i.d., 5m) coupled with a Phenomenex® C18 guard cadridge (4mm3mm i.d., 5m), chromatographic separations were conducted. As the mobile phase, a solution of hydrochloric acid water (0.01 M; pH 2.4) and methanol (15 : 85, v/v) was pumped at a rate of 1.2 mL•min1. 50 L was the injection volume. For the purpose of calculating the concentration of memantine hydrochloride, absorbances were measured at 282 nm.

Chromatography analysis condition for Donepezil hydro chloride

On a Phenomenex® C18 analytical column (150mm4.6mm i.d., 5m) coupled with a Phenomenex® C18 guard cadridge (4mm3mm i.d., 5m), chromatographic separations were conducted. The detecting wavelength was 268 nm, and the flow rate was set at 1 ml/min. The column received an injection of an 80 l sample.

Kinetics study

Kinetics of drug release is studied by plotting the data obtained from *in vitro* release in various kinetics models.

Zero Order Kinetics

The graph was plotted as cumulative % drug release Vs Time where the drug release rate is independent of its concentration (United States Pharmacopoeia 30 and National Fomulary 25, 2007).

$C = K\theta t$

Where,

$K\theta$ = Zero order rate constant expressed in units of concentration/time t = Time in hours.

First order Kinetic model

The graph was plotted as log cumulative % of drug remaining Vs Time, where release rate is concentration dependent (Korsmeyer RW, et al, 2007).

$\text{Log } C = \log C_0 - Kt / 2.3030$

Where,

C_0 = Initial concentration of drug K = First order constant

t = Time in hours.

Higuchi kinetics

According to Higuchi, the method by which pharmaceuticals are released from an insoluble matrix is square root time-dependent and depends on Fickian diffusion. Drug release percentage cumulative versus square root of time was used to plot the graph. (Baker RW and HS Lonsdale, 1974).

$Q = Kt_{1/2}$

Where, K = Constant reflection design variable system $t_{1/2}$ = Time in hours.

As a result, the drug release rate is inversely proportional to the square root of time. A dose form is thought to follow Higuchi kinetics of drug release if the plot produces a straight line and the slope is one.

Hixson-crowell erosion equation

It describes the drug release with changes in the surface area and the diameter of particles the data were plotted using the Hixson and crowell rate equation. The graph was plotted by cube root of % drug remaining in matrix Vs time (Ei-Arini et al, 1995).

0 t

$$Q^{1/3} - Q^{1/3} = KHCt$$

Where,

Qt = Amount of drug released in time t Q0 = Initial amount of drug in tablet.

KHC = Rate constant for Hixon crowell rate equation

Korsmeyer-Peppas equation

To find out the mechanism of drug release, it was further plotted in peppas equation as log cumulative % of drug released Vs log time (Michel de O et al, 2008).

$$Mt / M\alpha = Kt\ n,$$

$$Log\ Mt / M\alpha = log\ K + n\ log\ t$$

Where,

Mt / Mα = Fraction of drug released at time t K = Kinetic rate constant

t = Release time

n = Diffusion exponent indicative of the mechanism drug release.

When the release mechanism is unknown or there are multiple types of release phenomena present, this model is used to assess the release of pharmacological polymeric dosage forms. The slope of the log cumulative% of drug released vs. log time plot could be used to determine the n value.

In vivo Bioavailability Studies

The availability of the drug to the biologic system is integral to the goals of dosage form design and paramount to the effectiveness of the medication. Bioavailability study of the prepared tablets was assessed. Animal experiment was performed as per the protocol approved by the Institutional Animal Ethics Committee (160/1999/CPCSEA; Proposal Number 1127; Approved on 16.04.2015).

Animals

For the in vivo study, male Wistar Albino rats weighing 200–250 g were employed. Prior to the trial, the rats spent a week getting used to the temperature-controlled environment. Food and water were available to the rats at all times. The animals will be kept in 12-hour light/dark cycles during this week. The study began during the cycle of light. There are three animals (n=3) in each of the seven groups that were formed from the animals. The tablets were dissolved in distilled water and given to the rats via an oral feedtube. (Vinay pandit., 2012 and Tarek A., 2012).

Experiment

For the pharmacokinetic investigation, 21 animals are required. Seven groups of creatures were created. There are three animals in each group. Animals in group 1 were in charge. Reference standard (commercially available tablet) and orodispersible tablet of Donepezil HCl, respectively, were given to the animals in groups 2 and 3.

Reference standard (commercially available tablet) and orodispersible tablet of Galantamine HBr were administered to the animals in groups 4 and 5, whereas Memantine HCl and Galantamine HBr were administered to groups 6 and 7, respectively.

Group 1	Control (Sterile Water)
Group 2	Commercially available tablet of "Donepezil HCl" (CPD) (0.90 mg/kg bodyweight of animal)
Group 3	Orodispersible tablet of "Donepezil HCl"(DF36) (0.90 mg/kg bodyweight of animal)
Group 4	Commercially available tablet of "Galantamine HBr" (CPG) (0.72 mg/kg bodyweight of animal)
Group 5	Orodispersible tablet of "Galantamine HBr" (GF12) (0.72 mg/kg bodyweight of animal)
Group 6	Commercially available tablet of "Memantine HCl" (CPM) (0.900 mg/kg bodyweight of animal)
Group 7	Orodispersible tablet of " Memantine HCl" (MF24) (0.90 mg/kg bodyweight of animal)

Evaluation of Parameters

Rats' retro orbital plexuses were used to collect blood samples at 0, 5, 10, 20, 30 and 40 minutes after injection. The blood samples were drawn into purple-top EDTA vials and centrifuged for 20 minutes at 2000 rpm and 4 degrees centigrade. After centrifugation, insert 1.0 ml of plasma using the clean pipette technique into 1.5 ml of clean, brand-new Eppendorf tubes that have been labelled with a tracking number. The plasma will then be frozen at -20°C until being analysed. High Performance Liquid Chromatography will be used to measure the medication concentration in the blood plasma. By using a non compartmental model, the pharmacokinetic parameters were extracted from plasma concentration data. The pharmacokinetic parameters, such as the area under the plasma concentration time curve (AUC0-t), the highest plasma concentration (Cmax), and the time required to achieve the maximum plasma concentration, were calculated using Kinetica software (Version 5.1). (Tmax).

Stability studies as per the ICH guidelines

Stability studies performed on final batch as per ICH guidelines for 60 days at 40°C±2°C/75% RH±5%. Samples were withdrawn at 0, 3 and 6 months intervals and evaluated for their physical properties, hardness, disintegration time and *in vitro* drug release (Chatap.V.K et al, 2007).

CHAPTER FIVE

COMPARATIVE STUDY

Physicochemical properties

Table. 1 Comparison of physiochemical properties of Galantamine HBr, Memantine HCl and Donepezil HCl

S.No	Comparative parameters	Galantamine HBr	Memantine HCl	Donepezil HCl
1	Description	White to almost white powder	Fine white to off-white powder	White to off-white or slightly yellow crystalline powder
2	Taste	Unpleasant	Bitter	Bitter
3	Solubility	sparingly soluble in water, freely soluble in alcohol, acetone, and chloroform; less soluble in benzene	Freely soluble in ethanol and methanol, soluble in water, sparingly soluble in chloroform, and almost insoluble in acetone and isopropanol.	Freely soluble in chloroform, dichloromethane and in methanol, soluble in water, sparingly soluble in ethanol, n-butanol and in acetonitrile and very slightly soluble in acetone.
4	Melting Point	256 °C	258 °C	206 °C

Precompression study

Table .2 Precompression results of Galantamine HBr, Memantine HCl and Donepezil HCl

S.No	Parameter	Galantamine (GF)	Memantine (MF)	Donepezil (DF)
1	Bulk density	0.65 ± 0.02 to 0.72 ± 0.03	0.48 ± 0.02 to 0.54 ± 0.06	0.48 ± 0.04 to 0.57 ± 0.05
2	Tapped density	0.81 ± 0.01 to 0.89 ± 0.01	0.60 ± 0.02to 0.67 ± 0.02	0.52 ± 0.07 to 0.66 ± 0.08
3	Hausner's ratio	1.12 ± 0.05 to 1.36 ± 0.04	1.15 ± 0.02 to 1.24 ± 0.06	1.09 ± 0.04 to 1.24 ±0.07
4	Carr'x index	11.11 ± 1.19 to 26.96 ± 1.23	13.11 ± 0.67 to 19.04 ± 1.19	14 ± 1.19 to 20.1 ± 0.31
5	Angle of repose	31.08 ± 0.032 to 39.36 ± 0.024	33.09°±0.56to 39.14°±0.22	21.65° ± 1.42 to 30.6° ± 0.28

The granules of twelve different formulations from three drugs were evaluated for angle of repose, loose bulk density (BD), tapped density (TD), Compressibility index (CI) and Hausner's ratio. The granules were too cohesive to flow through the funnel.

S.No	Parameter	Galantamine	Memantine	Donepezil
1	Weight variation	101 ± 1.34 to 110 ± 1.45	98 ± 1.42 to 103 ± 1.49	98 ± 0.47 to 103 ± 0.31
2	Hardness	3.5 ± 0.2 to 5.0 ±0.26	2.4 ± 0.23 to 3.7 ± 0.16	2.4 ± 0.13 to 3.8 ± 0.65
3	Friability	0.16 ± 0.02 to 0.83 ± 0.03	0.25 ± 0.027 to 0.61 ± 0.041	0.33 ± 0.021 to 0.75 ± 0.033.
4	Thickness	1.84 ± 0.22 to 2.84 ± 0.16	1.2 ± 0.23 to 1.8 ± 0.21	1.2 ± 0.16 to 1.9 ± 0.06
5	Wetting time	45 ± 1.3 to 12 ± 0.9	40 ± 0.9 to 15 ± 0.6	32 ± 2.1 to 10 ± 0.6
6	Disintegration	49 ± 2.3 to 13 ± 1.4	38 ± 1.3 to 12 ± 1.3	33 ± 2.1 to 10 ± 2.3
7	Drug content	87 - 101%	96.3 to 101.4	96.41 to 99.86

The average weight, thickness, drug content, hardness, friability, disintegration time, and wetting time of the produced tablets were all measured in order to study these properties. The outcomes demonstrate that the product can be stable, accomplish the least amount of disintegration, and remain within the required range.

In vitro study

All three medication formulations have demonstrated that the drug release increases along with the disintegrant concentration. A subliming agent and an effervescent material were added to orodispersible tablets to boost the medication release rates. However, the drug releases from these tablets were found to increase with increase in the concentration of disintegrant and other ingredients used in the formulation. *In vitro* release of drugs is a direct function of its solubility in the dissolution medium. Based on the *in vitro* release study one formulation was optimized from each drug i.e. GF12, MF24 and DF36 formulations were given 99.7, 99.8, 99.9% of satisfactory release respectively.

Study	Galantamine HBr		Memantine HCl		Donepezil HCl	
	GF12	CPG	MF24	CPM	DF36	CPD
Disintegration (sec)	13±1.4	720±1.2	12±1.3	480±1.2	10±2.3	34±1.4
Hardness (Kg/cm^2)	5.0±0.26	4.3±0.32	3.7±0.16	4.7±0.23	3.8±0.65	3.2±0.18
Dissolution (%) in 20mins	99.7	60.2	99.8	65.9	99.9%	97.2

Based on the *in vitro* release study one formulation was optimized from each drug i.e. GF12, MF24 and DF36 formulations were given 99.7, 99.8 and 99.9% of satisfactory release respectively. All the three formulations GF12, MF24 and DF36 achieved least disintegration compared with commercial products (CPG,CPM &CPD) respectively. Hardness of these three formulations were satisfactory and all the results shows that formulated orodispersible tablets were superior than that of marketed product

Time in min	Galntamine HBr		Memantine HCl		Donepezil HCl	
	GF12	CPG	MF24	CPM	DF36	CPD
0	0	0	0	0	0	0
2	56.3	4.9	40.4	8.2	30.9	13.6
4	68.6	17.8	78.4	16.6	34.5	19.8
6	73.4	23.6	82.2	29.8	37.8	27.4
8	86.3	28.1	83.5	33.5	49.3	33.9
10	91.8	35.2	92.1	40.1	58.6	44.2
12	93.6	42.8	93	47.8	77.9	60.3
14	97.1	49.6	95.1	52.6	83.4	67.9
16	98.6	53.5	96.7	58.5	93.7	76.6
18	99.1	58.7	97.9	61.8	98.8	89.5
20	99.8	60.2	99.7	65.9	99.9	97.2

Based on the *in vitro* release study one formulation was optimized from each drug i.e. GF12, MF24 and DF36 formulations were given 99.7, 99.8 and 99.9% of satisfactory release respectively. All the three formulations GF12, MF24 and DF36 achieved least disintegration compared with commercial products (CPG,CPM &CPD) respectively. Hardness of these three formulations were satisfactory and all the results shows that formulated orodispersible tablets were superior than that of marketed product

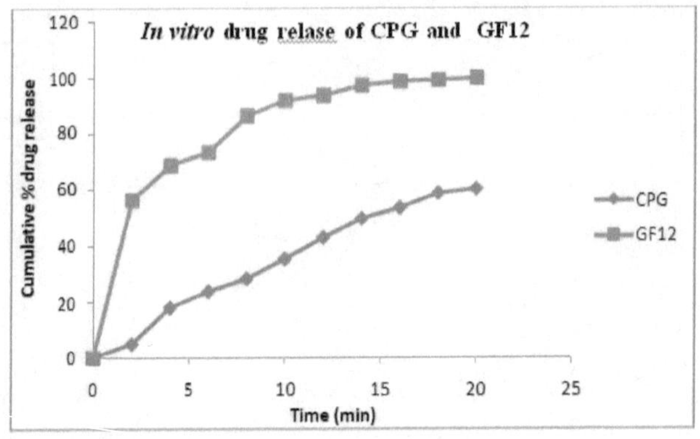

In vitro Drug Release of CPG AND GF12

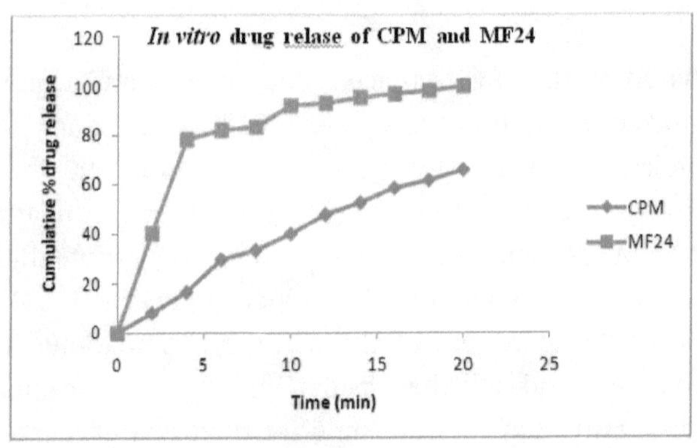

Fig 2.*In vitro* drug relase of CPM and MF24

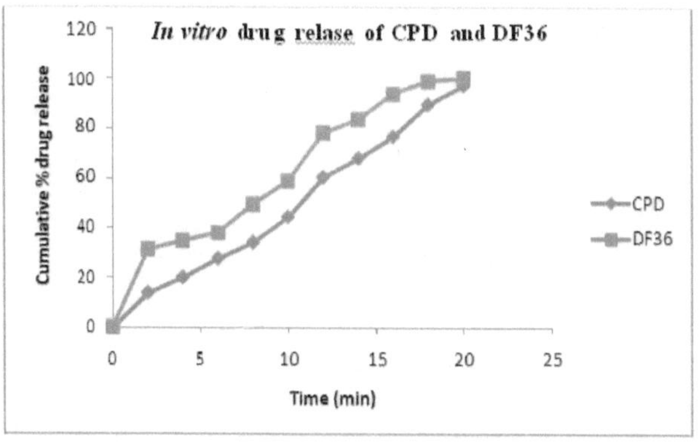

Fig 3.*In vitro* drug relase of CPD and DF36

In vivo study

The in vivo investigation was carried out on the optimised GF12, MF24, and DF36 orodispersible tablet formulations and compared with the commercially available CPG, CPM, and CPD formulations of the same medicines, respectively. Tmax was reached earlier. Comparing the ODT formulation to the conventionally marketed product, a higher C max was attained. The in vivo investigation was carried out on the optimised GF12, MF24, and DF36 orodispersible tablet formulations and compared with the commercially available CPG, CPM, and CPD formulations of the same medicines, respectively. Tmax was reached earlier. Comparing the ODT formulation to the conventionally marketed product, a higher C max was attained.

It was discovered that GF12, MF24, and DF36 were superior than their commercial versions. When compared to the other two formulations, GF12 and MF24, it was discovered that DF36 (donepezil HCl) performed better in terms of drug release, disintegration, and all other metrics.

CHAPTER SIX

SUMMARY AND CONCLUSION

Summary

This thesis deals with the investigations carried out by the writer with the objective of developing orodispersible tablet formulations for widely used Alzheimer's disease drugs Galantamine HBr, Memantine HCl and Donepezil HCl for the evaluation of their disintegration, drug release potential.

The primary scope and objectives of the research study are covered in the first chapter of the thesis. It explains why creating an appropriate medication formulation for the investigation's chosen drug candidates is necessary in particular.

In the second chapter of the thesis, the pathology, aetiology, and current therapies for Alzheimer's disease are discussed along with the notion of orally disintegrating release drug delivery system and its relation to oral drug delivery system.

The literature review for the studies that have been done so far on the development of ODT drug delivery systems and the most recent advancements for the chosen drug candidates are covered in Chapter 3.

Chapter 4 deals with brief plan of work. It clearly explains how the objectives of the work will be achieved.

The experimental methodologies used are described in depth in Chapter 5 of the thesis, specifically the Analytic hierarchy approach, preformulation investigations, and

ODT tablet formulation and evaluation, in vivo bioavailability research, and stability testing of the created formulations.

The experimental findings from the current investigation are covered in depth in Chapter 6 along with a thorough analysis of the findings supported by tables and figures. Among the significant results of the current investigations are the following: The developed ODT tablets exhibit acceptable pharmacopoeial characteristics, indicating that the method can be applied to scale-up studies. The drug release can also be significantly modulated by altering the component of the various superdisintegrants, effervescent substance, and subliming agents used in this study.

The created ODT tablets of the chosen medication candidates exhibit a suitable in vitro release profile, weight variation, and friability. The concentration of the disintegrant had a substantial impact on the behaviour in vitro. In general, a significant amount of the drug release was delayed by an increase in the disintegrant concentration. For the optimised batches of Galantamine, Memantine, and Donepezil over the course of 20 minutes, the cumulative percentage drug release from the immediate release orodispersible formulations was 99.7, 99.8 and 99.9, respectively.

The developed ODT formulations of Galantamine, Memantine, and Donepezil have demonstrated six months of stability under accelerated settings. The developed orodispersible pills could demonstrate oral disintegration. The ODTs medication created in this study will better sustain plasma drug levels, overcoming the limitations of conventional therapy.

The pharmacokinetic parameters of the three different formulations of Galantamine, Memantine and Donepezil were compared statistically by one way

ANOVA (analysis of variance) by using SPSS version 13.0. By using a one-way ANOVA, it was discovered that the pharmacokinetic parameters Cmax, Tmax, AUC, and t12 of the ODT formulations of Galantamine, Memantine, and Donepezil were significantly different from one another (p 0.001). These findings lead to the conclusion that the developed ODT tablets comprising Galantamine, Memantine, and Donepezil are stable, able to demonstrate orally disintegrating qualities, and practical for manufacture on an industrial scale. They can thereby increase drug release from the dose and, as a result, boost patient adherence to treatment management.

Future scope of the work

To further establish its potential and therapeutic efficacy, additional studies involving their suitability for long-term application, shelf life determination, bioavailability, and clinical investigations in large populations may be required.

Conclusion

The study's overall conclusion was that these improved formulations might work well for treating Alzheimer's disease. Additionally, these formulations meet all pharmacopoeial and non-pharmacopoeial standard requirements, and the approach can be regularly applied to an industrial process.

CHAPTER SEVEN

REFERENCES

Baker RW and HS Lonsdale: Controlled release; mechanism and rates in Controlled Release of Biologically Active Agents. Plenum Press, New York, 1974.

Banker GS, Anderson NR. Tablets. In: Lachman L, Lieberman HA, Kanig JL. *The theory and practice of industrial pharmacy*. Ed 3. New Delhi: CBS publishers and distributors; 2009, 171-196, 293- 345.

Bardelmeijer, H.A., et al., The oral route for the administration of cytotoxic drugs: Strategies to increase the efficiency and consistency of drug delivery. *Investigational New Drugs*, 2000;18(3) 231-41.

Bhagwati ST., Hiremath SN. and Sreenivas SA., Comparative evaluation of disintegrants by formulating cefixime dispersible tablets, Indian J. Pharm.Edu.Res, 2005; 39, 194-197

Blennow K, de Leon MJ, Zetterberg H. Alzheimer's disease. *Lancet* 2006 ; 29;368(9533) 387-403.

Bradoo R . Fast Dissolving Drug Delivery Systems.J. Am. Med. Asso.2001; 4: 27-31.

Chandira RM1, Venkataeswarlu BS, Kumudhavalli MV, Debjitbhowmik, Jayakar B. Formulation and evaluation of mouth dissolving tablets of the Etoricoxib. Pak J Pharm Sci.

2010; 23(2) 178-81.

Chang RK, Guo X, Burnside BA, Cough RA. Fast dissolving tablets. Pharm Tech, 2000; 24, 52-58.

Chatap.V.K, Sharma.D.K, Middha.A,Gupta.R.D, Saini.Shiradkar.M, Mouth disintegrating tablets of taste masked ondansetron Hcl Asian J. chem. 2007;19, 3455-3609.

Chun-Woong Parka,b, Dao-Danh Sona, Ju-Young Kima, Tack-Oon Oha, Jung-Myung Haa, Yun-Seok Rheec,*, Eun-Seok Parka, Investigation of formulation factors affecting in vitro and in vivo characteristics of a galantamine transdermal system, International Journal of Pharmaceutics, 2012; 436, 32–40.

Comoglu T, Inal O, Yaacoub HB. Formulation and in vitro evaluation of ketoprofen fast- dissolving tablets. Pharm Dev Technol. 2015; (23)1-8.

Cooper, J., Gunn, C., "Powder flow and compaction", In: Carter SJ, eds. *Tutorial Pharmacy*.

CBS Publishers and Distributors, New Delhi, India 1986, 211-233

Desai S1, Poddar A1, Sawant K2. Formulation of cyclodextrin inclusion complex-based orally disintegrating tablet of eslicarbazepine acetate for improved oral bioavailability. Mater Sci Eng C Mater Biol Appl. 2016; 1(58) 826-34.

Dixit, S., et al., Fast Dissolving Tablet-A Promising Approach For Drug Delivery: A Review.

Journal of Pharmacy Research, 2012; 5(3) 1508-1513.

Ei-Arini, S.K. and H. Leuenberger: Modelling of drug release from polymer matrices: Effect of drug loading. International journal of Pharmaceutics, 1995; 121(2) 141-148.

Fong Yen W1, Basri M2, Ahmad M1, Ismail M3 , Formulation and evaluation of galantamine gel as drug reservoir in transdermal patch delivery system., ScientificWorldJournal, 2015:495271.

Gadiko C1, Tippabhotla SK, Thota S, Battula R, Khan SM, Vobalaboina V., A Randomized, Crossover, Single-Dose Bioequivalence Study of Two Extended-Release Tablets of Donepezil 23 mg in Healthy Human Volunteers under Fasting and Fed States., Sci Pharm. 2013; 81(3)777-91.

Gauri, S. and G. Kumar, Fast dissolving drug delivery and its technologies. The pharma innovation, 2012; 1(2) 34-39.

Ghosh, T., A. Ghosh, and D. Prasad, A Review On New Generation Orodispersible Tablets And Its Future Prospective. International Journal of Pharmacy and Pharmaceutical Sciences, 2011; 3(1) 1-7.

Gohel M, Patel M, Amin A, Agrwal R, Dave R, Bariya N. Formulation design and optimization of mouth dissolve tablets of nimesulide using vaccum drying technique. AAPS PharmSciTech 2004;(5)1-6.

Ishikawa T1, Watanabe Y, Utoguchi N, Matsumoto M, Preparation and evaluation of tablets rapidly disintegrating in saliva containing bitter-taste-masked granules by the compression method., Chem Pharm Bull (Tokyo). 1999; 47(10)1451-4.

Kamer AR, Craig RG, Dasanayake AP, Brys M, Glodzik-Sobanska L, de Leon MJ.Inflammation and Alzheimer's disease: Possible role of periodontal diseases. *Alzheimers Dement*. 2008; 1(4) 242-255.

Keny RV1, Desouza C, Lourenco CF. Formulation and evaluation of rizatriptan benzoate mouth disintegrating tablets. Indian J Pharm Sci. 2010; 72(1) 79-85.

Khachaturian, Zaven S., and Teresa S. Radebaugh. Alzheimer's Disease: Cause(s), Diagnosis, Treatment, and Care. Boca Raton: CRC, 1996; 135 Print.

Khatavkar UN1, Shimpi SL, Kumar KJ, Deo KD, Controlled release reservoir mini tablets approach for controlling the drug release of Galantamine Hydrobromide., Pharm Dev Technol. 2012; 17(4) 437-42.

Kim JI1, Cho SM, Cui JH, Cao QR, Oh E, Lee BJ, In vitro and in vivo correlation of disintegration and bitter taste masking using orally disintegrating tablet containing ion exchange resin-drug complex, Int J Pharm. 2013; 455(1-2)31-9.

Korsmeyer RW, et al.: Mechanisms of solute release from porous hydrophilic polymers.

International journal of Pharmaceutics.1983; 15(1) 25-35.

Kumaresan C, Orally Disintegrating Tablet - Rapid Disintegration, Sweet Taste, and Li K1, Yang S, Study on novel galantaminehydrobromide sustained-release capsules and itsin vitro releasing property., Pak J Pharm Sci. 2014;27(5) 1621-26.

Liew KB1, Peh KK, Fung Tan YT, RP-HPLC analytical method development and optimization for quantification of donepezil hydrochloride in orally disintegrating tablet., Pak J Pharm Sci. 2013, 26(5) 961-6.

Liew KB1, Tan YT, Peh KK , Taste-masked and affordable donepezil hydrochloride orally disintegrating tablet as promising solution for non-compliance in Alzheimer's disease patients, Drug Dev Ind Pharm. 2015; 41(4) 583-93.

Liltorp K, Larsen TG, Willumsen B, Holm R, Solid state compatibility studies with tablet excipients using non thermal methods. J Pharm Biomed Anal., *2011*; 55(3),

424-428.

Lygia Azevedo Marques a, Ismail Maadaa, Frans J.J. de Kanter b, Henk Lingemana, Hubertus Irtha, Wilfried M.A. Niessena, Martin Gieraa,, Stability-indicating study of the anti- Alzheimer's drug galantamine hydrobromide, Journal of Pharmaceutical and Biomedical Analysis volume 2011; 55(1) 85–92.

Manikandan M, Kannan K, Thirumurugu S, Manavalan R. Design and Evaluation of Amlodipine Besilate and Atorvastatin Calcium Tablets. RJPBCS 2012; 3(1) 425-434.

Manikandan Mahalingam, Kannan Krishnamoorthy, Selection of a Suitable Method for the Preparation of Polymeric Nanoparticles: Multi - Criteria Decision Making Approach Adv Pharm Bull, 2015, 5(1), 57-67.

María J. Culzoni a, Ricardo Q. Aucelio b, Graciela M. Escandar c,*, High-performance liquid chromatography with fast-scanning fluorescence detection and multivariate curve resolution for the efficient determination of galantamine and its main metabolites in serum, Analytica Chimica Acta, 2012; 740, 27–35.

Martin RF. Effective pharmacologic management of Alzheimer disease. AJM. 2007; 120, 388–397.

MeyyaNathan S.N., Mathew Philip, and Suresh B., Spectrophotometric Determination of Baclofen in its Dosage forms, Indian Drugs, 1998; 35, 183-187.

Michel de O, Rossana B, and RC: Effects of filler-binders and lubricants on physicochemical properties of tablets obtained by direct compression: a 2 factorial design. Lat. Ameri. J. of Pharm. 2008; 27(4) 578-583.

Misra S1, Chopra K2, Sinha VR3, Medhi B, Galantamine-loaded solid-lipid nanoparticles for enhanced brain delivery: preparation, characterization, in vitro and in vivo evaluations., Drug Deliv. 2015; (25) 1-10.

Modi A and Tayade P. Enhancement of dissolution profile by solid dispersion(kneading) technique. AAPS Pharm. Sci. Tech, 2006; 7(3) 68-75.

Moorthi C, Kathiresan K, Reversed phase high performance liquid chromatographic method for simultaneous estimation of curcumin and quercetin in pharmaceutical nanoformulation. Int J Pharm Pharm Sci., 2013; 5(3), 622-5.

Nayak P, SM,Gopalkumar, Design and optimization of fast dissolving tablets for promethazine theoclate. Indian Drugs, 2004; 41, 554-6.

Olmez SS1, Vural I, Sahin S, Ertugrul A, Capan Y. Formulation and evaluation of clozapine orally disintegrating tablets prepared by direct compression. Pharmazie. 2013; 68(2) 110-6.

Postina R. A closer look at alpha-secretase. Curr Alzheimer Res. 2008; 5(2):179-86.

Prabhakar. V et al., Fast Dissolving Tablets: An Overview. International Journal of Pharmaceutical Sciences : Review and Research, 2012;16(1) 17-26.

Pragnesh patel, Anupkumar Roy, Vinod kumar SM, Martand kulkarni. Formulation and evaluation of colon targeted tablets of ornidazole for the treatment of Amoebiosis. International Journal of Drug Development and Research 2011; 3(1) 52-61.

Rajeev Soni. et al., Design And Development Of Quick Dissolving Tablet Containing Loratadine By Direct Compression Method.IJPCBS, 2013; 3(3) 771-800.

Rani Thakur, R. and A. Verma, Mouth Dissolving Tablets- Preparation Characterization and Evaluation:An Overview. Journal of Pharmacy Research, 2012; 5(2)993-1000.

Reisberg, Barry et al. Memantine in Moderate-to-Severe Alzheimer's Disease. *New England* Journal of Medicine, 2003 ; 3;348(14)1333-41.

Riedel, G., B. Platt, and J. Micheau. Glutamate Receptor Function in Learning and Memory. Behavioral Brain Research. 2003; 18;140(1-2)1-47.

Saaty TL. Decision making with the analytic hierarchy process. Int J Services Sciences 2008;1(1)83 – 98.

Sara Laserra a , Abdul Basit b , Piera Sozio a , Lisa Marinelli a , Erika Fornasari a , Ivana Cacciatore a , Michele Ciulla a , Hasan Türkez c , Fatime Geyikoglu d , Antonio Di Stefano. Solid lipid nanoparticles loaded with lipoyl–memantine codrug: Preparation and characterization, International Journal of Pharmaceutics 2015; 485, 183–191.

Sarfraz RM1, Khan HU2, Mahmood A1, Ahmad M1, Maheen S2, Sher M3. Formulation and evaluation of mouth disintegrating tablets of atenolol and atorvastatin. Indian J Pharm Sci. 2015 ;77(1)83-90.

Shah D., Shah Y., Rampradhan M. Development and evaluation of controlled release diltiazem hydrochloride microparticles using cross-linked poly (vinyl alcohol) Drug Dev. Ind. Pharm. 1997, (23) 567–574.

Shailesh Sharma. New generation of tablet: Fast dissolving tablet. Pharmainfo.net.

Shao-Jun Jing, Qing-Lian Li, Ye Jiang* , A new simultaneous derivatization and microextration method for the determination of memantine hydrochloride in human plasma, Journal of Chromatography B, 2016; 1008, 26–31.

Sheshala R1, Khan N, Darwis Y. Formulation and optimization of orally disintegrating tablets of sumatriptan succinate. Chem Pharm Bull (Tokyo). 2011; 59(8) 920-8.

Shirsand SB1, Suresh S, Jodhana LS, Swamy PV. Formulation design and optimization of fast disintegrating Lorazepam tablets by effervescent method. Indian J Pharm Sci. 2010; 72(4) 431-6.

Shirwaikar R., Shirwaikar A., Prabu L., Mahalaxmi R., Rajendran K.,Kumar C. Studies of superdisintegrant properties of seed mucilage of *Ocimumgratissimum*. Indian J. of Pharmaceutical sciences. 2007; 69(6) 753-758.

Shoukri RA1, Ahmed IS, Shamma RN . In vitro and in vivo evaluation of nimesulide lyophilized orally disintegrating tablets. Eur J Pharm Biopharm. 2009; 73(1) 162-71.

Shu T (2002). Studies of rapidly disintegrating tablets in oral cavity using coground mixture of mannitol with crospovidone. Chem Pharm Bull , 2000;50 (2) 193—198 .

Shukla D, Chakraborty S, Mouth Dissolving Tablets I: An Overview of Formulation Technology, Sci Pharm. 2009; 76; 309–326.

Soh JL1, Grachet M, Whitlock M, Lukas T . Characterization, optimisation and process robustness of a co-processed mannitol for the development of orally disintegrating tablets. Pharm Dev Technol. 2013; 18(1) 172-85.

Sreenivas, S., et al., Orodispersible tablets: New-fangled drug delivery system-A review. *Indian*

Journal of Pharmaceutical Education, 2005; 39(4) 177-185.

Tejvir K., Bhawandeep G., Sandeep K., Gupta G.D. Mouth dissolving tablets: a novel app to drug delivery. Int. J. Cur. Pharm. Res. 2011; 3(1)1–7.

Thies W, Bleiler L, Alzheimer's Association, Alzheimer's disease facts and figures. *Alzheimers Dement.* 2013;9(2) 208-45.

United States Pharmacopeia 24/NF19,The Official Compendia of Standards. Asian Rockville,

M.D. (Ed.), United States Pharmacopoeia Convention Inc, 2000, 1913–1914.

United States Pharmacopoeia 30 and National Fomulary 25. The United States Pharmacopoeial Convention,CD ROM, 2007.

Velmurugan R, Selvamuthukumar S, Manavalan R., Multi criteria decision making to select the suitable method for the preparation of nanoparticles using an analytical hierarchy process. Pharmazie 2011;66(11)836 -42.

Vinay pandit, Roopa S. Pai, Kusum Devi and sarasija suresh, *In vitro-in vivo* evaluation of fast- dissolving tablets containing solid dispersion of pioglitazone hydrochloride, journal of advanced pharmaceutical technology and research, 2012; 3(3), 160-170.

Woo FY1, Basri M2, Masoumi HR1, Ahmad MB1, Ismail M3 , Formulation optimization of galantamine hydrobromide loaded gel drug reservoirs in transdermal patch for Alzheimer's disease. Int J Nanomedicine. 2015; 5(10) 3879-86.

www.alz.org

www.medterms.com

www.webmd.com

Yıldız S1, Aytekin E1, Yavuz B1, Bozdağ Pehlivan S1, Ünlü N1. Formulation studies for

mirtazapine orally disintegrating tablets. Drug Dev Ind Pharm. 2015; (4)1-10.

www.ingramcontent.com/pod-product-compliance
Lightning Source LLC
Chambersburg PA
CBHW021122130726
47988CB00003B/1116